THE MAN WHO CREATED MERSEYSIDE FOOTBALL

THE MAN WHO CREATED MERSEYSIDE FOOTBALL

John Houlding, Founding Father of Liverpool and Everton

David Kennedy

ROWMAN & LITTLEFIELD
Lanham • Boulder • New York • London

Published by Rowman & Littlefield
An imprint of The Rowman & Littlefield Publishing Group, Inc.
4501 Forbes Boulevard, Suite 200, Lanham, Maryland 20706
www.rowman.com

6 Tinworth Street, London SE11 5AL

British Library Cataloguing in Publication Information Available

Library of Congress Cataloging-in-Publication Data

Names: Kennedy, David, 1961– author.
Title: The man who created Merseyside football : John Houlding, founding father of Liverpool and Everton / David Kennedy.
Description: Lanham : Rowman & Littlefield, [2020] | Includes bibliographical references and index. | Summary: "This biography of John Houlding, the principal figure in the creation of both Everton and Liverpool football clubs in the late nineteenth century, provides a comprehensive look into early professional football, breaking new ground by addressing the important role of football club ownership in the early history of the game"— Provided by publisher.
Identifiers: LCCN 2019057090 (print) | LCCN 2019057091 (ebook) | ISBN 9781538141236 (paperback) | ISBN 9781538141243 (epub)
Subjects: LCSH: Houlding, John, 1833-1902. | Liverpool Football Club—History. | Everton Football Club—History. | Sports team owners—Great Britain—Biography. | Soccer—England—Liverpool—Biography. | Businessmen—Great Britain—Biography. | Politicians—Great Britain—Biography. | Soccer—Great Britain—History—19th century. | Liverpool (England)—Biography.
Classification: LCC GV942.7.H66 K46 2020 (print) | LCC GV942.7.H66 (ebook) | DDC 796.334092 [B]—dc23
LC record available at https://lccn.loc.gov/2019057090
LC ebook record available at https://lccn.loc.gov/2019057091

♾ ™ The paper used in this publication meets the minimum requirements of American National Standard for Information Sciences Permanence of Paper for Printed Library Materials, ANSI/NISO Z39.48-1992.

CONTENTS

PREFACE

Football supporters the world over are aware of the great rivalry that exists between the two giants of Merseyside football: Everton and Liverpool. It is one of the great rivalries of sport; the teams' on-field encounters are an often fiercely fought, physical battle for local supremacy. Football aficionados will know that, like that other great conflict existing between Internazionale and A.C. Milan, the Merseyside football rivalry was created out of a split within one club that gave rise to the other—a clash over matters of governance at Everton FC resulting, in 1892, in the emergence of Liverpool FC. The two clubs from the city of Liverpool subsequently went on to dominate the English game, amassing twenty-seven English top-flight titles between them, more than any other city in the country.

What perhaps isn't as well known is that one man was responsible for the rise of both clubs: the former lord mayor of Liverpool, John Houlding. A brewer and Conservative politician, Houlding was a polarising yet fascinating figure who cast a huge presence not just in sports entrepreneurship but also in politics and the functioning of the local state on Merseyside. The absence of a study dedicated to one of the most important historical figures in the creation of English football is an anomaly. The primary objective of this book, therefore, is to correct this omission and broaden our knowledge and understanding of this man—'King John'—a local figure who had a global cultural impact.

ACKNOWLEDGMENTS

I am indebted in particular to Dr Peter Kennedy and Mr John Campbell for their advice concerning this work. Their expertise on identity politics and Merseyside football, and the social significance of football more generally, was invaluable to me in the construction of this book. I would also like to thank my family for their consideration and support throughout, and I dedicate this book to them.

Without the expertise of the staff at the following institutions, the archival material required to complete my research would have been much more difficult to unearth—if not impossible—and I offer them my gratitude: the British Newspaper Library, Collindale, London; Brotherton Library, University of Leeds; Companies House, Cardiff; Grand Lodge Library, London; Harold Cohen and Sydney Jones Library, University of Liverpool; Liverpool Public Record Office; Liverpool Probate District registry; Public Record Office, Kew; and the Probate Department, Principal Registry of the Family Division, High Holborn. I also thank the following individuals, who provided particular guidance on archival sources: Mike Braham, secretary of Southport Liberal Association; Geoff Brandwood, chair of Liverpool West Derby Conservative Association; Rebecca Coombes, the Library and Museum of Freemasonry, Freemason's Hall, London; Lee Le Clerque, secretary of the North West Brewers' and Licensed Retailers Association; photographic advice, Mr Ged Thompson; and David Beckingham, author of *The Licensed City: Regulating Drink in Liverpool, 1830–1920*.

INTRODUCTION

John Houlding was the man who pioneered professional football in the city of Liverpool. His financial input, first at Everton Football Club and then at Liverpool Football Club, provided the launchpad for the establishment of two nationally and internationally known sporting organisations. Winning between them twenty-eight English titles and ten major European trophies, Liverpool is England's most successful football city. Houlding's legacy to football is immense.

Before his involvement in the game, Liverpool was a relative backwater for association football. Its progress was stunted by the dominance of rugby—the code which transfixed the ranks of the middle class, the class of people that had been at the fore of the foundation of football clubs elsewhere in England. By the 1880s, Liverpool's football status was still minor in comparison with that of many towns and cities in Lancashire, Yorkshire, and the Midlands; its best teams were no match for England's best teams. In Lancashire especially, rugby's dominance had been broken by the creation of the Lancashire Football Association, and teams like Bolton Wanderers, Burnley, and particularly Blackburn Rovers were attracting great interest. It was teams from Blackburn—first Olympic and then Rovers—that broke the dominance in the FA Cup (the premier football competition) of southern England's gentlemen amateur teams such as the Old Etonians, Old Carthusians, and Wanderers FC, who comprised alumni from elite public schools. Merseyside football needed its spark, and it received it with the charismatic Houlding, a popular civic figure capable of widening the appeal of the game from its limited social base, with the added impetus of investing cash from his brewing business. This was manna from football heaven. First Everton FC, then Liverpool FC took full advantage of his association. By the time of Houlding's death in 1902, both clubs had reached the pinnacle of the English game by securing a league title apiece. His place as the founding father of professional football in the area, therefore, is assured.

Both Everton and Liverpool football clubs have huge followings (Liverpool FC's chief executive claimed in 2018 that their club had 'several hundred million fans around the world', perhaps as many as seven hundred million),[1] and the cultural legacy Houlding bequeathed via these organisations is of enormous importance. But his establishment of Merseyside's football giants isn't the whole of his story. Rising from the poverty of his childhood in the old Parish of Liverpool, a cow keeper's son, John Houlding was the embodiment of the self-made Victorian man. The great seaport of Liverpool rose in unison with imperialist triumph, and the enormous trade that flowed through it created opportunity for men of capital who could invest in merchant vessels taking their cargo in and out of its vast, state-of-the-art docks. It also created the opportunity for a man like Houlding, not only as a brewer who could make his fortune in quenching the thirst and drowning the sorrows of the growing population of a booming city but also as a man with a flair for organisation. Houlding came to the fore in Liverpool public life as a councillor and poor law guardian as the city struggled to maintain its balance under the weight of the rapid population growth which had placed great strain on its housing stock and health and welfare institutions.

Houlding was a prominent politician and a towering figure in the creation of the local state in Merseyside. Both a Conservative and an interventionist, he had concluded that the only way to maintain civic order and social stability was to deploy a municipal reform programme to reduce poverty and ill health. In his lifetime, he influenced everything from the administration of workhouses and the running of hospitals to the creation of a sanitation regime to overcome the city's appalling hygiene issues, and he made a serious attempt to deal with the issue of orphaned children in Liverpool. In fact, when Houlding died, the tributes paid to him focussed on this, his broader civic legacy, rather than his football legacy.

Where the efficient running of the local state was concerned, a profile emerges of John Houlding as a pragmatic reformer. In so called 'imperial affairs', though, Houlding was stridently conservative; a man committed to the monarchy, to the state, to the union of Britain and Ireland, and, above all, to the maintenance and expansion of the British empire. Houlding was aggressively opposed to any political force or social group perceived to be intent on undermining the status quo. Radicalism in all its forms—reformist or revolutionary—was firmly in his crosshairs. Houlding, as a self-made and well-to-do man, was determined to protect the life he had carved out for himself and his family, and he waged battle all of his adult life for the system that allowed him to prosper. He was, though, not without contradictions in this respect, and the complexity of his character surfaces in the telling of his story. He was a businessman, and also the president of several trades unions; a champion of workers' political representation, though passionately opposed to independent working-class politics. John Houlding was somewhat of an enigmatic character.

Obviously, the major interest in John Houlding as a subject is due to his contribution to the world of football, and in particular, his role in the creation of Liverpool FC. Any study declaring itself to be a considerate assessment of his life and work must also recognise and acknowledge this primary interest in him, and an in-depth assessment of his involvement in football is incumbent upon a biographer. That said, Houlding the football entrepreneur—his motivations and his decision making—cannot be understood without having knowledge of Houlding the family man, the businessman, and the politician. His business and political life, in fact, became entangled in dramatic fashion with the Liverpool football scene on more than one occasion. In this biography, therefore, a balanced view has been sought. Houlding's important role in local politics and in the creation of the local state on Merseyside are intertwined here with the crucial role he played in the area's football development.

John Houlding was, of course, a man of the times he lived through. Put simply, the opportunities that presented themselves to Houlding were influenced by the fast-changing physical environment around him and the spirit of the age he lived through. The dramatic physical, economic, and technological development of the city of Liverpool in the second half of the nineteenth century must have been wondrous to a young man nurturing an ambition to get ahead in life. To witness Liverpool being transformed from a large northern English town to one of the greatest metropolises in the world would have been a huge stimulus to his strategic thinking about how he could play a part in this transition and take advantage of it.

Houlding was viewing at close quarters the creation of a powerful maritime city-state. Just as Venice and Genoa had in an earlier period, Liverpool was in the process of becoming a flourishing trading center, dominating commerce between Western Europe and the rest of the world, but with the added velocity of the technological innovations in transportation and communications of the industrial age. This process remodeled the environment Houlding grew up in dramatically. From being just another provincial English town, Liverpool, on the strength of its trade, became a city of conspicuous wealth. In the second half of the nineteenth century, Liverpool created more millionaires than in any city outside of London; more than were created in Manchester and the large towns and cities of the Midlands and Yorkshire combined,[2] its economy sustained a population (almost seven hundred thousand by the 1890s), greater than in any other British city apart from the capital.

All cities will change to one degree or another over the course of decades. But the change to Liverpool over the seventy years of John Houlding's existence was intense. The physical environment was revolutionised, the changing skyline of Liverpool reflective of civic confidence—and, more than that, a boastfulness. There was a proliferation of neoclassical, gothic, and renaissance public buildings; a statement from the city fathers that they were not to be regarded as comparable to any other provincial English city. This was no idle boast. With over 2,500 listed buildings of special architectural, historical, or cultural significance, Liverpool has been dubbed England's finest Victorian city.[3] Huge infrastructural projects were also undertaken to service the city's rapidly increasing population: transportation networks criss-crossed Liverpool by the end of the century. In 1869, Liverpool was the first borough in Britain to secure an Act of Parliament to establish an extensive tram network; an internal rail system constructed in the 1870s linked up all outlying suburbs with each other and the city centre. In 1886, the Mersey Tunnel, the world's oldest underground railway, was built, linking Liverpool to the Wirral Peninsula; and in 1897, the Liverpool Overhead Railway, running the six-mile length of Liverpool's dockland from north to south, was opened. The face of Liverpool altered beyond all recognition.

Liverpool's meteoric rise as a maritime economy and the enormous wealth it generated, and its civic leader's willingness to commit to ambi-

tious architectural and infrastructural projects, were the stimulating conditions that John Houlding and others like him—those capable of spotting
an opportunity to create value—would find inspiration from. Beyond this
psychological stimulus towards entrepreneurship, the material development of the city was vital to the establishment of football clubs, in particular. Simply put, if Liverpool had not been the powerful and complex city
it became, with its huge population, its vast wealth trickling down to an
army of clerks, managers, and professionals, and beyond them to a large
skilled and semiskilled workforce affording the cost of entertainment and
travel; without its advanced transportation systems to efficiently convey
tens of thousands people, it is doubtful that any entrepreneur—even a
determined and gifted one as John Houlding proved himself to be as a
brewer—could have pioneered not one but two successful, mass-supported football clubs. It was certainly a feat unmatched in England outside of London, and only in Scotland in Glasgow was there any real
parallel to be found, in the creation of the mass-supported Glasgow Rangers and Glasgow Celtic. In fact, by the early 1890s, Liverpool was host to
three professional clubs: Everton, Liverpool, and Liverpool Caledonians,
and one existed in nearby Bootle. To paraphrase Karl Marx: men like
Houlding made their own history, but not as they pleased. The material
conditions for success needed to be in place.

ORGANIZATION OF THE BOOK

This biography is a chronological, 'cradle to the grave' study and reveals
the events and people central to the telling of John Houlding's life story.
That story begins with the decision made by his parents, who were farm
labourers, to leave their village, Heskin in West Lancashire, in order to
seek work in Liverpool. The first chapter describes John's parents' lives
when arriving in inner-city Liverpool, the hardship endured by John as a
boy, his school life, and his early introduction into the world of work,
both as a helper in the family dairy business and then later at the Liverpool customs house. John's eventual settling into an industry that would
become the source of his wealth and power—the brewing industry—is
then discussed. We witness the quick-learning Houlding ascending
through the ranks of Clarkson's Brewery, first as a young man carrying
out the back-breaking work of a brewery drayman, and in later years

promoted in fairly quick time from brewery foreman, to head brewer, to brewery manager. In the course of this career, John marries and starts a young family. Houlding was not settled, however, and struck out on his own in business creating his own brewery company, 'Houlding's Sparkling Ales'. The chapter concludes when—business success assured—John Houlding breaks through to the elite social scene, symbolised when he and his own family move to their exclusive villa, Stanley House.

Chapter 2 takes up the story of John's arrival in Everton, the district that would become strongly associated with his name. A description is given of the rapid urban development of Everton, and an understanding is offered concerning this huge district's importance within the borough (then city) of Liverpool. Houlding's determination to translate his new-found wealth into social and political capital is discussed by highlighting his power grab on a variety of institutions in the district, including the local Conservative Party, the local Poor Law Union, trade union bodies, and in his patronage and creation of a number of sports clubs. By the chapter's end Houlding is portrayed as a man now in control of his own fiefdom ('King John of Everton') and in a ready position to transcend the local to become a national figure of importance.

In chapter 3, though, we leave aside for the time being Houlding's ambitions to convert local political influence for parliamentary honours in order to focus on his overtures to the most well-known and important institution in Everton, its football club: Everton FC. It was an organisation Houlding had initial difficulty gaining a foothold in, but involve himself he did. Eventually it too succumbed to his attentions when he was made its president. We see how Houlding's wealth and resources attracted the improving but financially insecure club into his orbit of influence and eventual control. Here, the Anfield stadium is mentioned for the first time, and an appreciation is offered of the means by which the stadium was secured for Everton FC—a transaction that would prove to be hugely controversial and lay the basis for the eventual split of the club and the emergence of Liverpool FC. Much of the chapter, however, is given over to highlighting the rise of the club from park team to English League champions, which is charted against the backdrop of Houlding's hugely expensive outlay on stadium infrastructure and player personnel. We also see, however, the developing rupture within the club between its president and the membership as issues of club governance begin to tear the club apart.

Having built up a stronghold in the politically important district of Everton (its city councillor from the mid-1880s and chair of the district Conservative Party), Houlding had made himself a strong favourite to become an MP for the Everton constituency. However, Houlding's plans to enter the Palace of Westminster were all but wrecked in the early 1890s after a series of challenges to him in his civic seat from forces committed to ending his electoral dominance in Everton. Chapter 4 chronicles these events and analyses the forces halting Houlding's forward momentum. Houlding, as a brewer, faced huge opposition from a surging temperance movement intent on carrying forward their 'purity campaign' and to upbraid and unseat any prominent member of the drink trade holding public office. A challenge to Houlding in Everton also came in the form of independent working-class political organisations, which had been gaining momentum for many years within the district. Although Houlding repelled this opposition to hold onto his municipal seat, the city's Tory leadership were persuaded that to run Houlding as a parliamentary candidate in Everton or elsewhere in Liverpool would be too much of a risk.

Houlding's political ambitions may have been dashed, but he still had other cards to play. Chief amongst them was his involvement with Everton, the country's top football club. Taking up the issue of division discussed in chapter 3, chapter 5 details the events that lead to the breakup of Everton FC—a breakup on the basis of fundamental disagreements over how the club should be run, but which also exhibited bitter personal animosities and a twist of political intrigue. Out of the ashes of the old club, Houlding created Liverpool FC. Unlike Everton FC, Liverpool was Houlding's own organisation. He set it up on a firm business basis to be run by a coterie of trusted political allies and men who worked for him at the West Derby Union. The remainder of chapter 5 is the telling of the story of Liverpool's first decade of existence, culminating in the club becoming English League champions in 1901.

The successful foundation of Houlding's new football venture, it is argued in chapter 6, provided the basis for his 'Indian Summer'. This penultimate chapter highlights a number of achievements secured by Houlding in what proved to be the final years of his life. Chief amongst these was a return to the political centre stage on becoming lord mayor of Liverpool in 1897—although, and as with most other things with John Houlding, there was controversy attached to it: his appointment being opposed by his old foes in the temperance movement. Houlding also completed his lifetime service to freemasonry by being installed as the grand deacon of England, which elevated him to 'the craft's' Grand Council—Houlding had made it into a very exclusive club of monarchs-in-waiting, the great landowners of the country, and captains of industry. This late period of success was crowned with Liverpool FC's championship-winning season of 1901–1902.

The final chapter begins with the events surrounding Houlding's death in Cimiez, France at the age of sixty-nine in March 1902. The public response to the passing of one of the juggernauts of Liverpool society is outlined and examined. The remainder of the chapter considers the impact Houlding made in his life, his significance in terms of legacy. This evaluation is split into two broad sections. First, there is a discussion of his many achievements in public life; his contribution to the city's political culture, the local state and, of course, to football. Second, there is an evaluation of Houlding's character when the question is posed: 'What type of man was John Houlding?'

I

FROM TENTERDEN STREET
TO ANFIELD ROAD

The John Houlding story begins not in Liverpool, but in rural West Lancashire, with the decision made by the recently married Thomas and Alice Houlding at the end of the 1820s to leave their village in Heskin near Chorley and make the twenty-five-mile journey to Liverpool to seek employment. Thomas and Alice were part of a pattern of migration of landless agricultural workers who were being pulled into the orbit of the booming Liverpool economy, attracted by the lure of better wages and steady employment. With agrarian workforce wages under pressure—in many cases supplemented by parish relief—the decision to leave Heskin for a more rewarding standard of living must have seemed like an obvious one to make. Census records underline the drift into Liverpool by people like the Houldings. By the mid-nineteenth century, over 13 per cent of those living in Liverpool and its nearby satellite towns were born in rural Lancashire and Cheshire.[1]

As part of this rural exodus from Lancashire, Thomas and Alice Houlding would have felt every bit the economic migrants making their way into Liverpool as the Welsh and Irish—national groups particularly associated with migration into Liverpool at that time. Thousands of these Lancastrian migrants settled in Liverpool's semirural hinterland, in places like Altcar and Formby, supplying their labour to arable crop farmers and doing much the same work as they had back in their own villages. Others, like Thomas and Alice Houlding, made their way to the borough of Liverpool instead. Arriving there in the late 1820s, they became cow keepers, servicing the local population with fresh dairy produce such as milk and butter. By the early 1830s, they had well and truly put down their roots in Liverpool and were now parents to two boys: John and William Houlding.

CHILDHOOD

John Houlding was born in August 1833 at 19 Tenterden Street, less than a mile from the River Mersey in the heart of the old parish of Liverpool. His parents were Anglican, and John was baptised at St Martins Church of England chapel, a short hop across the main thoroughfare, Lime Kiln Lane, from Tenterden Street. At that time, land to the south and west of the family home extending down towards the docks was being subject to dramatic population increase with courts, cellars, and dilapidated terraced housing on the verge of being overcome with the sheer scale of the influx of migrants into the port town. The neighbourhoods in the north of the parish of Liverpool where the Houldings lived had experienced a three-fold increase in population between 1801 and 1841.[2] Looking east, though, the land rising gently, and then precipitously, towards the township of Everton was still semirural.

As a cow keeper, John's father, Thomas, was therefore well situated to be able to graze his livestock on available common land *and* be within walking distance of selling his produce to a large number of people. Before the days of refrigeration, food was eaten fresh. The solution to delivering fresh dairy produce to customers was to bring cows to the centre of large towns and cities. And hundreds of cow keepers were needed to supply Liverpool's growing demand. Cow keepers came in the hundreds to Liverpool; many from nearby West Lancashire, as the Hould-ings had done, but also from as far away as the Lake District counties of Cumberland and Westmorland, eighty to a hundred miles away. Typical-ly, a small cow-keeping operation such as Thomas Houlding's would have had two or three cows, which would be milked early in the morning and then driven to a stretch of common land to graze for the day. The morning's milk would then be taken in churns from street to street in a cart, or slung over the shoulders in a yoke to be ladled out to customers. This choice of occupation would not have been a cheap venture either. Cow keepers had the annual cost of licensing and registering their business under the Public Health Act of 1800, which sought to curb the spread of disease in towns. Also, there was the cost to consider of replacing cattle stock. Once a cow had fallen below producing a profitable yield in terms of gallons of milk per day it would need replacing and new stock paid for, along with transportation fees from the countryside (usually Liverpool dairymen went to the farms of the Lake District for their cattle). It can be said, then, that Thomas Houlding had displayed an adventurous spirit in moving on from his old life as a farm labourer to his new one as the owner of a small business enterprise in a large city. This commitment to entrepreneurship would no doubt have been a huge influence on the young John Houlding.

The family business most certainly influenced the course of John's childhood, as the young Houlding brothers became their father's assistants—a common practice of the day. This initial foray into the world of work was an extremely tough one for a boy. As the elder brother, John would have had to rise at five or six o'clock in the morning in order to help milk the cows, clean out the cow house, and, later in the day after school, help his father with the cattle drive back from the grazing fields on the slopes to the east of their neighbourhood. This would have been followed up by more door-to-door sales of the family's dairy produce in late afternoon and early evening. To say the least, this was a challenging schedule for a child. Punishing workloads and the sacrifice of time would become a feature of John's adult life, and these earlier experiences in the small family business were the bedrock for it.

Though counting on their sons' labour to keep their business operational, Thomas and Alice Houlding also saw schooling as important. John attended the local Bond Street Church of England free school situated between Lime Kiln Lane and Vauxhall Road, a short walk from Tenterden Street. Later, aged eleven, he travelled further afield to attend Liverpool College in Shaw Street, Everton—his first link with the district that would become synonymous with his name. Liverpool College (or 'the Collegiate' as it is traditionally known in Liverpool) was a newly opened school when John attended it in the early 1840s. It was something of a coup for his parents to have him enrolled there. Formally opened by the future prime minister, Liverpool-born William Ewart Gladstone in 1843, the Collegiate consisted of lower, middle, and upper schools. The middle and upper schools were attended by boys looking to use their education to embark on careers in the professions, or to prepare for higher education (in particular, with a view to gaining a place at a college in either Cambridge or Oxford universities). It is safe to say that those careers would have been seen as beyond the reach of a cow keeper's son living in mid-nineteenth-century inner-city Liverpool. The lower school, where boys could study with the objective of gaining literacy and mathematical skills to get on to the bottom rung of the ladder of a business, was more in keeping with the realistic ambitions for the son of Thomas Houlding.

Despite the narrower remit for boys entering the college's lower school, the young John Houlding could not have been anything other than influenced by his academic environment. He spent two of his formative years at the college between the ages of eleven and thirteen, mixing with the sons of the upper middle classes and the merchant aristocracy of Liverpool. The experience must have opened his eyes to the possibilities of a life now unfolding before him. The college was a seedbed for an aspiring generation of political leaders—local and national—more especially those identifying with the Conservative Party. Two of John Houlding's contemporaries at the Collegiate were Thomas Royden and Arthur Bower Forwood, future leaders of the Liverpool Conservative Party and MPs for Liverpool constituencies. Other Conservative luminaries who attended the college were Sir Charles Petrie, Robert Hampson, George Kyffin-Taylor, and Austin Taylor. This clutch of Old Lerpoolians (as the college's graduates were known) would have great influence on the city's political life in the second half of the nineteenth century, as would John Houlding.

THE WORLD OF WORK

With the consent of his father, John decided to curtail his education at the Collegiate in order to take up an opportunity that had presented itself. Thus began John's first job outside of the family business: as a messenger at the imposing neoclassical customs house building on Liverpool's increasingly impressive waterfront. The founding of a customs house in Liverpool was something that the city's fathers had long petitioned the United Kingdom Treasury for. The function of a customs house was to oversee the import and export of goods into and out of the country, collecting a customs duty for this service. Securing permission to build and operate one added significant prestige to a port, stimulating growth in the local economy with the building of more docks and the creation of ancillary industries which would service the flow of cargo traffic. Other significant United Kingdom ports at the time, such as Dublin, Edinburgh, and Bristol—ports by the early decades of the nineteenth century that were beginning to be left behind by Liverpool's preeminence in international trade—had their own customs houses and Liverpool Corporation were determined to establish theirs, at all costs. In 1827, they received permission from the Treasury to go ahead and build one after agreeing to commit the then-enormous sum of £175,000 for its construction. From this it can be gleaned that employment at the Liverpool Customs House was a prestigious first job for John Houlding to have. For a young man to have the promise of a long career stretching ahead of him was unusual in a town where casual employment was largely the norm.

Though the position of messenger sounded like a menial position, it certainly was not. Messengers were one of a number of customs staff employed to oversee and scrutinise the huge amount of imports and exports needing to be cleared through the excise system. Messengers acted as a link between the various class of clerks and the traders who had presented themselves to make the required payment of duties. Good organisational skills, confidentiality, and a suitable level of literacy and numeracy were prerequisites for this post. A description of the young Houlding as having 'a receptive intellect and a sense of probity and disposition'[3] underlines that this young man's temperament was suited to the task at hand.

The customs house employed a number of young men to assist outdoor customs officers (or 'searchers') whose job would be, as the name suggests, to roam the docks checking out cargo in the holds of ships, on goods trains, and on wagons. John Houlding's job, therefore—predominantly in-house, clean, warm, and safe—was superior to the jobs many young men at the port would have been forced to take up. It was a position which quite conceivably could have been a stepping stone to becoming a clerk, the respectable trade of the Liverpool middle-class gentleman. Undoubtedly, for a young man from the run-down parish of Liverpool, the customs house job was a golden ticket out of the precarious world of casual employment. It also handed him the chance to escape his hazardous inner-city environment. Perhaps with this knowledge, Houlding looked up with growing interest at the suburban housing developments which had sprung up on the slopes towards Everton, visible from

his family's Tenterden Street home, planning his way upwards and on-
wards.

However, this career path was not to be. John's first foray into paid
work was brought to an abrupt halt when the cattle plague (bovine tuberculosis) hit Liverpool's milk producers in the late 1840s. It decimated the
family dairy business, and John was duty bound to 'put down his pen in
order to aid his parents'.[4] Rapid urbanisation was to blame for the outbreak. Though bovine tuberculosis was a familiar problem for cow keepers like Thomas Houlding, it thrived to epidemic proportions because of
changing environmental conditions. By the end of the 1840s, the grazing
space enjoyed by Thomas Houlding's and other cow keepers' cattle at the
periphery of the city had shrunk to hardly any available common land at
all. The district of Everton where Thomas had previously made his daily
cattle drive to and from was in the process of being settled by house
builders, who had begun to transform the area from grassland to terraced
streets full of 'two-up, two-down' houses. As a result, cow keepers like
him were forced to turn their own yards into permanent quarters for their
cattle. Instead of the daily ritual of exercise, fresh air, and eating fresh
grass, urban cattle had little or no free movement, spending their days in
cramped conditions with changes to their diet from fresh grass to food
waste. All of this maximised the spread amongst herds of mycobacterium
bovis, a respiratory infection passed via droplets from cow to cow and
affecting their lungs. However, and despite John Houlding's return to the
family dairy business to lend a helping hand, his father's herd had to be
destroyed. The milk they were producing was unfit for human consumption, and particularly deadly for infants. It was a catastrophe for consu-
mers and producers alike. The upshot of its deadly outbreak in Liverpool
in the 1840s was that the Houlding family would need to look elsewhere
for work to make ends meet.

It is worth pausing at this point and appraising the environmental
conditions that John Houlding was facing in his youth. Mid-nineteenth-
century Liverpool was, to say the least, a dangerous place to be. A city
dubbed 'the Blackspot on the Mersey', its rapidly growing population
(increasing from 165,000 in 1831 to 376,000 in 1851), densely packed
often into substandard houses and courts with scarcely any sort of clean
fresh water or sanitation, were the sitting victims for wave upon wave of
killer epidemics. An addition to preexisting migration from Lancashire
and Wales was the tens of thousands of desperate Irish migrants fleeing

the ravaging effects of famine in their homeland and whose presence exacerbated the already chronic overcrowding in Liverpool. Diseases such as tuberculosis, typhus, smallpox, and cholera took a terrible toll, costing thousands of lives and severely affected the health of tens of thousands of other Liverpudlians. The Liverpool cholera outbreak of 1849 alone claimed well in excess of five thousand lives.

These environmental conditions had a devastating effect on average life expectancy. To put it bluntly: if your hometown was Liverpool, you had a lot fewer years of life to look forward to than if you lived elsewhere in the country. In the inner districts of Liverpool—which is where John Houlding and his family lived—average life expectancy in 1850 was twenty-seven years, falling to twenty-five years in the following decade. By comparison, the average life expectancy for the rest of England and Wales for those two periods were forty-two years and forty-one years, respectively. And the higher than national average mortality rate Liverpool faced was suffered across all social classes. In 1842, social investigator Edgar Chadwick calculated that, compared with parts of the south of England where tradesmen had an average life span of forty-one years and the professional classes fifty-two years, in Liverpool the respective figures stood at twenty-two years and thirty-five years.[5] Clearly, the young John Houlding was faced with an ongoing existential threat.

An intelligent, resourceful, and ambitious young man would have needed no telling that he had to escape his immediate environment if he was not to suffer the fate many people in inner-city Liverpool would meet. With his father's business having failed, there must have been a strong motivation and sense of urgency to get on in life and make the most he could of his talents. His saving grace was that he lived in a city that (however dangerous) was also experiencing exponential economic growth. Liverpool was the gateway to an expanding British Empire, the port through which trade between Britain and Africa and the Americas flowed. The volume of trade at the port of Liverpool grew almost tenfold between 1800 and 1850, from 450,000 tonnages of shipping to 4 million, due to the massive demand for food, raw materials, and, above all, the manufactured goods the British economy was producing and which the rest of the developed and developing world yearned for.[6] This expansion of trade gave rise to a bustling port economy. The *Illustrated London News* described Liverpool as 'The New York of Europe, a world city rather than merely British provincial'.[7] For anyone with guile and the good health to exploit its many opportunities, there was a fortune to be made there. These were qualities the savvy and robust Houlding had in spades, and, eventually, take his opportunity he would. However, with the family dairy business in ruins, the young man would have to place his personal plans on hold to again answer the call of his parents and contribute to the family income.

The 1851 census records tell us that the eighteen-year-old John Houlding's occupational status was now 'auditor at home'. His time spent in the customs house having equipped him with a certain level of balance-sheet skills, it appears he was now earning money as an independent bookkeeper of sorts, perhaps charging the many local tradesmen a fee for his auditing. However, this work was very much a sideline. By this stage, John Houlding's career had already taken a dramatic turn away from the white-collar path he had been groomed for. His father, Thomas, had exchanged his own failing cow-keeping business for employment at Clarkson's Brewery in Soho Street, on the district border between the parish of Liverpool and Everton. At this point, John Houlding was working as a porter at the Liverpool Exchange railway station, but when his father secured him a position as a labourer at Clarkson's Brewery he joined him there. It proved to be an important turning point in his life, and the first step on the way to securing his wealth, power, and influence.

The next two decades of John's life were taken up in a variety of jobs at Clarkson's Brewery. His first job of any responsibility, though, was working as a drayman. This tells us something of the young Houlding's physical prowess. In the world of nineteenth-century employment the job of a brewer's drayman was seen as a particularly physically demanding occupation. Their principal job was to load up the dray (a low, open, horse-pulled cart) with casks full of beer to deliver. The weight of these casks could range from the 110lb firkin (a quarter barrel), to the 220lb kilderkin (half barrel), to the full barrel weighing over 400lb, which would have to be loaded onto and off the flatbed dray when delivering to public houses, or else to the port to be loaded on barges or railway goods trains for transportation elsewhere away from Liverpool. The drayman's day could begin as early as four in the morning at the stables preparing their team of two or three horses. Once on the road, deliveries could last to as late as ten o'clock at night. This was a six-day-per-week job, and even Sundays could partly be taken up cleaning stables.

Status went with the job, though: in their traditional white topcoat and red peaked hat, the brewery drayman was looked upon as something of a champion of the working-class community. They were customarily to the fore in street protests of the eighteenth and nineteenth centuries, viewed as a strong-arm praetorian guard. They were not usually known, however, for their radical politics. The satirical magazine *Punch* noted that draymen were among the first to enroll as special constables in April 1848 to protect towns from Chartist demonstrations.[8]

An occupation that relied so much on physical strength often came at a price. The physical wear and tear of the job over many years frequently induced skeletal change. It was typical for a drayman's spine and ribcage to have to adapt to the colossal loads they were tasked with lifting and carrying. The destruction of cartilage and bone compacted into an ossified 'shelf' upon which casks could be borne. No doubt the physical toll on the drayman impacted on Houlding too, and perhaps it is no coincidence that he became an organiser and eventual president of the Liverpool Carters' Association, the representative body of the trade. However, Houlding was not going to sacrifice his mind and body to shifting casks around the city for any longer than he had to. Houlding had the drive and ambition to better his position, and he was intent on rising through the ranks of the brewery he worked for.

Clarkson's Brewery was in the process of becoming one of the largest brewing companies in Liverpool. It would eventually have over eighty tied public houses, including two of the grandest hotels in Victorian Liverpool—the Crown in Skelhorne Street and the Midland in Cases Street—and it had extended its operations by the 1870s to the point where it had acquired other breweries. Its proprietor, William Clarkson, represented the type of man the young Houlding sought to emulate: rich and politically connected. Clarkson lived at the Priory, a mansion in a leafy suburb of south Liverpool. Clarkson's Brewery proved to be a fantastic learning environment for Houlding to gain an understanding of the brewing industry and William Clarkson was a role model for him.

Houlding was first promoted to the position of brewery foreman. This was a job that linked the workforce (stablemen, coopers, maltsters, etc.) to the brewery manager and, via him, to the head brewer. It was a senior position and an impressive testament to the status and credibility of a young man in his early twenties. The character needed to be a brewery foreman is described in an article on labour relations within the brewing industry in the nineteenth century:

> The foreman should be carefully selected, if possible having a better standard of education than those under them; they should be paid well; made responsible for their own men and be in direct contact with the brewer. . . . He should be made responsible for good time keeping, and above all be able to make accurate records of work done. The foreman should be regarded as if he were a sergeant, and treated as such.[9]

His relatively tender years aside, Houlding's combination of imposing physical stature (and the respect gained with having experience with the very toughest side of brewing work as a drayman) allied to his college education and white-collar work experience at the customs house, made him an ideal foreman. He had already acquired a knowledge of hierarchies and how to work within them.

In 1856, after four years as brewery foreman, a chance for promotion came along when Clarkson's head brewer left his position. This was a step up for John, but not entirely a leap into the unknown. The task of brewery foremen was to work closely with head brewers on issues of quality control over the product, so a level of knowledge of the brewing process was gained before his taking up of what was undoubtedly the key job at the brewery. If that all sounds like an informal and improvised way of operating a business, that is because breweries were still, by the mid-decades of the nineteenth century, very much places where the 'practical brewer' (that is, informally trained on the job, and learning the methodology of brewing by observing the work of the previous head brewer) still held sway. This was a period before the introduction of brewing processes that would cater to the changing patterns of consumption. Basically put, the beer-tasting public later began to demand a more refined beverage, and this went hand in hand with developing industry techniques that allowed the use of sugar, raw grain, and malt substitutes to create a variety of different flavours. At that point, brewing passed into the hands of a new generation of brewers with scientific and technical training—in particular, to industrial chemists. These were changes Houlding would later embrace in his own business by packing his son William off to university in order to study industrial chemistry. In the 1860s, however, men without formal training like Houlding were more typical of those becoming head brewers: men who had come through the ranks and who were astute enough to learn from others how to make quality beer. There was also the added bonus of a rent-free house that went with the job of brewer at Clarkson's, which would be very useful for John given the changes taking place in his private life.

On 20 July 1856, at the age of twenty-three, John Houlding became a married man. His wife, Jane Lowe, was seven years his senior. Jane was the daughter of a farmer who had settled in Liverpool from Thornton, a village eight miles north of the city. The Lowe family, as farm owners, would have had greater status than Houlding's own family who were from farm labour stock. Houlding in later life would boast of his own family's 'Yeoman' heritage in West Lancashire, a claimed lineage to ancestors owning a small landed estate. [10] The reality, though, was that for John Houlding, a young man from an inner-city district of Liverpool, marriage to Jane would have represented a rise up the social scale, one in keeping with the recent upgrade of his own social status as head brewer at one of Liverpool's largest breweries. Victorian society was finely graded and signifying messages sent out via the choice of a spouse were recognised by one's peers as a declaration of status. This is not to pass harsh judgement on Houlding or suggest his feelings towards Jane were purely instrumental, it is merely a statement of fact regarding the times he lived in. There were informal laws revolving around marriage that any ambitious young man or woman would have been keen to observe. As the Liverpool Courier later recalled: 'Very early in life (John Houlding) was fired with the ambition to better his position'. [11] After marriage, Houlding lived with his wife in his new tied house just a few yards away from the Soho Street brewery he worked in. However, they later moved to their own city centre apartment on North John Street where the couple's first child, Alice-Margaret, was born in 1860. At the age of thirty-four, Jane was, for the standards of the day, a relatively old first-time mother (average age of mothers in England and Wales having their first babies at this time was twenty-two years). Three years later, John and Jane became parents for the second time when their son, William, was born.

The added responsibility of family life and providing a future for his children incentivised John to move further up the hierarchy at Clarkson's if the chance offered itself. Houlding had organisational skills in dealing with the brewery's employees and a knowledge of all stages of the production process, including head brewer. He had a holistic understanding of how a brewery ran and the quality of taste, aroma, and texture that was required in order to make it a competitive product. Houlding was a brewery manager in waiting, and it didn't take long for William Clarkson to recognise that fact and appoint him to the position. As brewery manager, Houlding was again asked to increase his capabilities to the point where he had to be able to grasp the logistics not only of how to control the smooth running of the brewery, but also to forge working relationships with people outside of Clarkson's in the supply chain. Dealing with suppliers of the various ingredients that went into brewing beer was key. Houlding needed to be able to keep costs down and quality up. He also had to oversee the brewery's tied house estate: interviewing for potential tenants and working closely with solicitors to secure the granting of licenses for Clarkson's public houses.

The general maintenance of the brewery was also part of a brewery manager's remit: determining when repairs and upgrades needed to be made to existing machinery and infrastructure. On top of this, Houlding needed to think of ways to make the brewery more profitable; expanding the business by securing more customers, perhaps by appropriately identifying advertising campaigns for Clarkson's range of beverages, and devising cost-saving measures in the production process, or in the delivery of beer. By his late twenties, Houlding had expert knowledge in how to run a brewing business. He was paid a salary of £200 per annum by William Clarkson, such was his value to his employer. This was an annual wage far higher than most skilled manual and skilled nonmanual workers would have made. For example, in 1871, average annual earnings for school teachers were £97 per annum; printers earned £80 per annum; skilled engineers £94 per annum. Houlding's income was more comparable with those of salaried white-collar workers, such as commercial clerks and civil servants. [12]

Houlding had already begun to financially plan for the future, having joined the St Anne's Building Society in 1858. In later life, he underlined the significance of that move when speaking to the Co-Operative Benefit Building Society: 'At the age of twenty-five I first became a member of a building society, and it was from that day I date my success'. [13] By 1864 Houlding had saved his first £100. By 1870 he had amassed £900. [14] Inside a decade, Houlding had risen from drayman to the key position of head brewer in Clarkson's Brewery. But he was still an employee. The overall strategy and decision making (and profits) remained in the hands of the owner, the brewery's founder, William Clarkson. Houlding wanted it all: to not only control a business, but to own and control *his* business. To do this he needed to strike out on his own, and having secured the capital to do so, that's exactly what he did.

HOULDING'S SPARKLING ALES

At thirty-seven, Houlding held a position of authority in a secure job which earned him a very good salary. The safe bet for him would have been to sit tight, content to be William Clarkson's top man and in control of a major Liverpool business, while all the while steadily building up a tidy sum of money in his building society account as a nest egg for the future. If Houlding wished, he could have had a respectable life in the suburban districts away from inner-city Liverpool, well away from the hubbub of the low-lying dockland districts. The separation of ownership and control at Clarkson's gave him status as being part of the managerial revolution: occupying a key mediating position between capital and wage labor—something Houlding was well equipped for. However, as with the decision to abandon his plans for white-collar respectability and take on the physically demanding work of the brewery drayman, he again chose to shift gears, backing himself to make the right decision—this time with the higher stakes of making the right decision not only for himself but also his family.

Houlding's first foray into independent trading was to buy a number of public houses, with the intention of reinvesting profits from them in an as yet to be purchased brewery. In the rolling out of this plan, however, Houlding had an early setback. The Liverpool Licensing Committee blocked his application to open a new public house on Everton Brow, not far from the Soho Street address of Clarkson's Brewery, because there was already an established public house just ninety yards from the proposed location.[15] As a former brewery manager with experience of dealing with the Licensing Committee, the refusal to gain a license to set up shop in Everton Brow would not have come as a surprise to him. He knew the organised forces of the Liverpool temperance movement would be vigilant on the granting of another license in a locality already catered to. However, Houlding knew that he would eventually get his way, as the brewing industry usually did in Liverpool. This was the era of the 'free trade' in liquor licenses. Beginning in 1861, magistrates in Liverpool gave the go ahead for the deregulation of licenses in order to allow the market rather than the courts to effectively police the number of public houses. In cases like Houlding's first application, where there was a reasonable impediment to setting up a public house, the court would act to deny a license. However, the majority of applications during this free-trade period were allowed, and the number of public houses in Liverpool rose dramatically. In the six-year period between 1861 and 1867, another four hundred pubs were built in the city.[16] Undoubtedly, this era of relaxation in licensing regulation was a factor in Houlding's decision to leave William Clarkson's employment and go it alone.

It has to be said that Houlding's profession was an extremely controversial one. Becoming a brewer made one as many enemies as friends in late nineteenth-century Liverpool. The city had gained the unwanted title of England's capital of drunkenness. To suggest that there was an over-abundance of opportunities to drink would be an understatement. In 1874 there were almost two thousand public houses in Liverpool—a figure that represented over one-fifth of all public houses in all the towns and cities of northern England put together.[17] Having 'a pub on every corner' was not a tribute, but a jibe at the city. Its coroner, Clarke Aspinall, had once declared that the only part of the clock many Liverpudlians knew 'was the closing hour of the public house'.[18] It was also argued that where drunkenness went, so too did crime, and Liverpool's crime statistics tended to back that belief up. In 1875, Liverpool's population represented 2 per cent of the population of England and Wales, but it accounted for over 10 per cent of all indictable crimes.[19] And crime wasn't the only byproduct of drink. The city's lamentable level of squalor was said to have its roots in the oversupply of pubs and off-licenses, which were predominantly found in districts with the worst sanitation. Drink, it was argued, discouraged prudence and propriety and encouraged idleness and poverty. Liverpool's reputation nationally took a hammering over these conditions, which forced a debate in the city over the brewing industry's role in an unfolding social disaster and cause for acute civic embarrassment. The city fathers' desire was for Liverpool to be seen as one of Europe's great cities. Its magnificent neoclassical public buildings were a statement to that end, but this darker side to the municipality was a concern; it projected a less than welcome alternative image. 'There were two very different Liverpool's in evidence', one historian explains, 'one the projection of the aspirations of the city's grandees, their wealth set in stone in some of the country's finest mid-Victorian buildings; the other the grim reality of insanitary, cheaply constructed housing, with streets that in the population quickly became haunts of crime'.[20] In late nineteenth-century Liverpool, there would be a battle royal between the brewing industry and a determined temperance movement intent on shackling it; but for Houlding, this was a battle for another day.

In the meantime, he persevered with his plan to gain public house licenses in the district of Everton, and his fresh applications were granted. He set up three pubs in quick succession on Breckfield Road in the neighbourhood of Saint Domingo. The jewel in the crown of his portfolio of properties was the establishment in 1871 of a public house on Oakfield Road: the Sandon Hotel—a public house which would play a pivotal role in the establishment of the city's football scene. Situated a stone's throw from Anfield Road, the Sandon Hotel was a rather grand affair, catering to a newly established upper-working-class and lower-middle-class community. Besides functioning as a public house, it boasted a number of bedrooms for paying guests, a billiard room, a large function room for hire, and a bowling green at the rear of the premises with attached club house. The latter facility would become the headquarters of the Everton Bowling Club and, eventually, the changing area for the team from Everton Football Club. The name chosen by Houlding, 'the Sandon', refers to Viscount Sandon, a Liverpool Conservative MP and minister in the Pitt Government of the early nineteenth century. The exterior of the Sandon Hotel has an assortment of ornate tiles with masonic symbols on its exterior. John Houlding had recently been initiated into freemasonry, having joined Everton Lodge in 1871, and freemasonry would play an important role in Houlding's life (a subject returned to later).

At this time in Liverpool there was a growing trend towards the control of public houses by the large, so-called 'common brewers', such as Peter Walkers and Greenall Whitley, who sought to distribute their beer exclusively through 'free houses' (public houses not owned by the brewery but tied to them by the supply of their beer). Given his knowledge and experience in the industry as a manager-head brewer, Houlding was determined to resist falling into the trap of being a mere retailer of another brewer's beer. His investment in a small number of public houses allowed what the *Liverpool Courier* described as 'the prudent accumulation of capital' to establish in the winter of 1871 his own brewery in Tynemouth

Street, Everton.[21] The name of this addition to the Liverpool brewing scene: 'Houlding's Sparkling Ales'.

At first, he had only one employee, his friend (and future Liverpool FC director), John James Ramsey, whom he had trained to become head brewer. However, his portfolio of public houses quickly generated Houlding profits which he reinvested into the brewery, buying more plant and machinery and employing more workers. His plan was coming together. In business terms, John Houlding had arrived. His new brewery was to be the base upon which his fortune would grow, supplying his own beer to his own outlets and taking all of the profit. Eventually, it would also produce for him the wherewithal to gain a commanding foothold in another industry which was about to take off commercially, one which would vie with the drink industry for the affections of the city's working classes: professional football.

With his brewery up and running, and the addition of more public houses to his growing 'stable' of drinking establishments, Houlding's future, and that of his growing young family (Alice-Margaret and William had been joined by an adopted child, Isabella) was in the process of being secured. This was underlined by John Houlding's latest change of address. When Houlding had made the move from Clarkson's Brewery he was living at Robson Street, Everton, the owner of a terraced cottage in a largely skilled, working-class neighbourhood. His next move was to a house on the district border between Everton and Anfield, and it was a step up into another social world. In 1874, John Houlding acquired half an acre of land on Anfield Road for the sum of £635 and commissioned a builder to construct his family's new home.[22] Two years later, the bespoke 'Stanley House' was ready for occupation. Now the owner of a sumptuous villa adjacent to the exclusive Stanley Park, this was a grand statement from a confident man nearing the height of his powers. With an imposing neogothic turret giving unobstructed views over the parkland to the rear, Stanley House was (and remains) an impressive three-story property. The land Houlding had purchased in 1874 was also large enough to build a stables and coach house to the side of the villa. There were more than twenty rooms, with marble fireplaces a dominating presence in many of them. High ceilings were bordered by ornate coving carved into the shape of leaves and fruit. A billiard room was set aside at the top of the villa for Houlding and his guests to enjoy.[23]

Stanley House was in the neighbourhood of Breckfield—an area where the original merchant settlers of Everton had erected their mansions a half a century earlier when it was largely unspoiled land. Stanley House and other new-build villas had been added to the Breckfield estate in the 1860s and 1870s when it became fully attached to the Liverpool urban sprawl. The Houldings were residents in a very well-to-do neighbourhood, one where men like Henry Tate of the famous sugar-refining business Tate and Lyle had placed down roots. Tate lived in 'Woodlands', and he was typical of the upper-middle class residential makeup of those living in the mansions abutting Stanley Park. Anfield Road may have been barely a couple of miles away from Tenterden Street, the street of John Houlding's birth, but it was a world away in terms of the quality of life it had to offer.

* * *

Houlding's gamble to set up in business had paid off. After the struggles of his earlier working life, he had made it. He stood as the embodiment of the successful rags-to-riches Victorian man, and the public were becoming familiar with his name. One reason for this was that his philanthropic efforts were frequently reported in the local press. One *Liverpool Mercury* report, for example, described Houlding's generosity in inviting to Stanley House girls and boys who were, or had recently been, patients at Stanley Hospital for a tea party. (This relationship with the hospital lasted for the rest of Houlding's lifetime; indeed, Houlding, when at Everton FC and then Liverpool FC, made Stanley Hospital the official charity of his football clubs.) Another story carried in the press was of Houlding donating to the 'Aged and Deserving Poor Fund', the *Liverpool Mercury* reporting that two hundred hot-pot dinners had been paid for and handed out in Everton in his name.[24] With such largesse, John Houlding was effectively announcing himself to the public as a man of means and a benefactor; shaping his public image to one befitting his developing status as a businessman. Houlding was also moving in elite circles within the brewing industry and looking to play his part in defending it against the lively temperance movement in the city. To this end, he helped set up the Liverpool and District Brewers and Spirits Merchants Association alongside major local and regional brewery owners such as Robert Cain, Daniel Higson, James Tarbuck, and his old boss, William Clarkson.[25]

Now a man in his early forties, Houlding was in a hurry to make a name for himself beyond brewing. From the comfort of his suburban seat at Stanley House he would steadily increase his wealth and look for more commercial opportunities. But he would also seek to translate his financial success into social and political capital. Still enormously ambitious, the large and influential district of Everton he both resided in and traded from was to be fashioned to his will in order to achieve his personal objectives. Everton would soon provide John Houlding with a major power base within Liverpool.

2

CONQUERING EVERTON

A relatively self-contained village community of fewer than five hundred people in 1801, Everton had few strong social or economic links with the burgeoning port town of Liverpool to its west. However, its gradual settlement by Liverpool merchant families eventually brought the district within the orbit of influence of Liverpool. The growing connections between the two townships were formalised in 1835 with the inclusion of Everton (as well as the townships of Kirkdale, Toxteth, and Edge Hill) into an extended Liverpool borough ('Greater Liverpool' as it was alternatively known). The population of Everton at that point was approximately six thousand.

From being a semirural idyll at the beginning of the nineteenth century, there occurred a gradual urbanisation of the township from the 1840s to the 1860s when land on its 'border' with the parish of Liverpool became part of the urban conurbation that stretched up from the port town's dockland districts. Sir James Picton, a local architect and historian, described Everton's colonisation in disapproving language, portraying the urban transformation of much of Everton between the 1840s and 1860s as being carried out by 'philistines' in the garb of builders: 'Building commenced about 1840, and gradually and with accelerating steps the spade and pick-axe attacked the slopes of the hill side; the click of the chisel and the ring of the trowel were borne on the breeze to the villas above, giving warning of their coming fate; fashion and exclusiveness winged their way to more retired localities and a few years witnessed the metamorphosis of a rural suburb into a densely populated town'.[1]

From 1801 to 1851 the parish of Liverpool's population rose from 77,000 to 258,000. Those with the means to put some distance between themselves and the teeming masses of dockside Liverpool made their way to neighbouring Everton, which was also attracting migrants from outside of the city. With a population of 70,000, the district was transformed by the 1860s into a huge dormitory for those whose livelihoods depended on the port. Eventually its population would peak at 120,000 in the first decade of the twentieth century, by some way the largest district in the city of Liverpool.

By the time John Houlding arrived in the district as a resident in the mid-1870s, its urbanisation was virtually complete. Almost all of the old township had been developed with a mixture of artisan cottages and larger semidetached and detached middle-class residences. The transformation from township to 'dormitory town' occurred so rapidly, however, that the new population of Evertonians lacked a strong civil society: a network of identity-enhancing organisations that could galvanise them and give them a sense of place. Sociologists would describe this problem in terms of 'anomie': people uprooted from their previous close-knit communities who struggle to bond with their new surroundings. That same sense of estrangement would have been true also for those settling Everton at this point. And integration was made more difficult by the bewildering mixture of people from a variety of different backgrounds who settled in Everton. Census records point to a population stratified along occupational and ethnic lines. The majority of Evertonians were working class, and, for sure, would had some affinity through this. But there were gradations within this class between skilled manual workers (such as engineers and shipwrights), and skilled nonmanual workers (such as clerks and custom officers). There were also semiskilled workers (for example, postal workers and railway guards), and not an inconsiderable number of manual labourers (dock workers and merchant seamen had a sizeable presence in the district). Everton was not an area with one large employer or industry that would impose an obvious sense of identity based on employment. That *was* the case in some areas of the city, such as Wavertree and Kirkdale where large numbers of railway workers were typical, or in the districts of Vauxhall and Scotland Exchange where dock labouring was overwhelmingly the occupation of the working class. Everton's workforce was much too disparate for a unity based on 'us versus them', employer versus employee. Added to the complexity within the Everton working-class population, there was a substantial and equally diverse middle-class presence in the district. Professionals such as doctors and teachers, and a commercial class made up of accountants, merchants, and brokers, resided in large numbers, more especially in the Breckfield neighbourhood of Everton.

Besides Everton's occupational diversity there was likewise a sense of difference engendered by the ethnic profile of the district. In 1871, only 2 per cent of those living in Everton were born there. Although a large minority of the new Evertonians were born in the nearby parish of Liverpool, the majority hailed from towns and villages in Lancashire and other English counties further afield (some as far away as Northumbria and Kent), and from the so-called 'Celtic-fringe' nations of Ireland, Scotland, and Wales.[2] In fact, in pockets of the district ethnic enclaves were formed. The Welsh were an ethnic group particularly associated with Everton to the extent that Welsh language newspapers were sold in shops there. The prominence of the Welsh community is underlined by the words of the earlier mentioned Sir James Picton, who describes parts of Everton where 'placards in the Welsh language may be seen on the walls and Welsh newspapers in the shop windows. The sharp click and guttural intonation of the Cambrian dialect is heard from many a cottage door'.[3] Irish Catholics had also settled into the Everton Village area of the district which abutted the parish of Liverpool. The growing number of Roman Catholic churches and schools built in that neighbourhood from the mid-nineteenth century bears testimony to their presence (much to the chagrin of the colony of Ulster Protestants who had also made Everton Village and the close by Netherfield neighbourhood their home turf).

It is true that there were craft and ethnic-based mutual societies in Everton, typically found in Victorian cities, offering intra-group unity of sorts, but all-embracing organisations which might have given the district some sense of broader cohesion were thin on the ground and rather weak. One such organisation formed in the 1870s was the 'Everton Brotherhood'—a charity describing itself as 'non-sectarian'. However, it was a short-run affair and there were no similar attempts made in the same vein.

This was fertile territory for a man like John Houlding, intent on building a power base, to enter into. These Evertonians were his type of people: first- and second-generation migrants, just like his own family were. He knew what motivated them and the way that they viewed the world. They craved stability, respectability, and identity. Houlding's objective was to satisfy those impulses and profit by it. To this end, he would gradually exert his control over (and, indeed, create) a number of organisations that would be utilised to 'fly the flag' for the district *and* to cement his reputation locally.

A NATURAL CONSERVATIVE

One organisation Houlding would utilise in this quest was the Conservative Party. Houlding was a committed true-blue Tory, fiercely and tribally so. But why was this? After all, he was not from a well-to-do background—born into a tough and dangerous inner-city environment and living a precarious existence dependent upon the fortunes of his father's small cow-keeping concern—and the Conservative Party of his day was closely associated with the propertied classes and its members viewed as reactionaries against progressive reform. Indeed, later in life Houlding was a man who involved himself with workers' organisations, demanding higher wages and better working conditions for the men he represented. He would not appear, therefore, to have been a likely candidate to become a leading member of the local Tory Party. So why did John Houlding become such a forceful evangelist for the Conservative cause?

In explaining this apparent anomaly the first thing to point out is that, if John Houlding had been of a mind to place his political allegiance elsewhere other than the Conservative Party in Liverpool, there would have been no appropriate alternative political home to deposit it. There was no Labour Party, and there would not be one until near the end of his life. The forerunners to the Labour Party who offered independent working-class-based politics were mostly utopian and socialist in nature and dominated by middle-class intellectuals. They were not parties of the urban masses, and certainly not a suitable home for an ambitious man like Houlding, whose style was populist and who favoured practical solutions to the everyday problems faced by ordinary people.

The main opposition to the Conservative Party in Liverpool were the Liberal Party, but they were not a good fit for Houlding for a number of reasons. Historically, the Liberals were mistrusted in Liverpool; their backing for the abolition of slavery in the eighteenth century, and their later backing in the 1860s of the northern states in the American Civil War over the slave economy states of the south, hit hard a Liverpool economy which had made vast profits from the transit of slaves and the trading of cotton. The Liberals had taken up a principled stance, but not one which endeared them to the local working class whose livelihood depended on trade through the port of Liverpool. 'A creature of stunted growth', wrote one historian about the Liverpool Liberal Party. 'On a number of issues the Liberals seemed careless of local interests'.[4]

One such issue concerned religious freedom. The Liverpool Liberals were a political party identified with supporting the rights of Roman Catholics; an unpopular move in a city where there was a sizeable population of Ulster Protestant migrants, mass Orange Order membership, and where Protestant firebrands such as the Reverend Hugh McNeile had great success in agitating the local population with a fierce brand of 'no-Popery'. Liberal support for the reestablishment of the Catholic Church in 1850 (reestablishing the full hierarchy of the Catholic Church in England), and later, under Gladstone's leadership, their adoption of the policy of Home Rule for Ireland, sealed their electoral fate for the best part of the nineteenth century in Liverpool and made the Tories an unbeatable force there. In an effort to become more competitive, the Liberals turned towards informal electoral pacts with the Irish Nationalists, coalescing their forces to defeat the Tories in municipal wards (Liberal and Nationalist candidates either stood aside to maximise the chances of municipal seat success or stood on a joint ticket); an association considered by sections of the Liverpool working class as, at best, unpatriotic.

The Liberal Party were never going to hold an attraction for John Houlding. Regardless of his attitude to Roman Catholicism, which will be addressed later, above all Houlding was an imperialist, and any political party truckling (as he would have seen it) to forces threatening the integrity of the empire—which is how Irish Home Rulers were viewed by the Tories—would have been given short shrift and a wide berth. This point is hammered home by Houlding's own words on the matter of the Liberal Party and foreign policy. In 1885, looking ahead to that autumn's General Election in which the Conservatives were hoping to topple the Liberal Government, Houlding addressed a rally of Liverpool Tories at Hooton Park in Cheshire: 'I hope that every Englishman and Irishman in the city will fight for those who uphold the interests and honour of the British Empire, and not again allow the honour of England to be trailed in the mud by a government who had been friendly to every country but their own. That government has degraded the old flag of England more than it has ever been degraded in living memory. With regard to colonial policy some men say "perish the colonies", but if we lost them we will become a second or third-rate power'.[5] (An impassioned plea, no doubt delivered in his fist-pumping demonstrative style of public speaking. A description of Houlding's style of oratory was given in the *Liverpool Mercury*: 'Every public speaker of eminence has a mannerism in gesture, and when Mr Houlding was scaling rhetorical heights he emphasised periods by waving his left arm, with fist clenched, up and down, with the force you see represented in the sign over a goldbeater's shop'.)[6]

Houlding was a reactionary in the historically specific sense of that word: a man opposed to the radicalism which challenged the social order of his age. In the course of his political career, he would return to the theme of 'radicals' and 'radicalism' time and time again. It could accurately be described as an obsession with him. In the eighteenth and nineteenth centuries radicalism was a force that threatened the traditional way of ordering society. Its targets were unreformed monarchies and any form of government that stood in the way of greater political democracy and national self-determination. Houlding's formative years were influenced by reports of convulsions to the old order throughout Europe, more particularly in the 1840s when a series of revolutions rocked the continent's ruling classes. In Britain, there was a demand for greater democracy too, giving rise to the mass working-class Chartist movement which demanded universal male suffrage and other electoral reforms. In Liverpool, the bread riots of 1855 and the sporadic strikes at the port would have seemed like foreboding signs of anarchy. And while Liverpool was not a hotbed of violent political organisation, it did have a tradition of radical reformist organisations such as the Hampden Club, a pressure group for parliamentary reform, and the Concentric Society, advocating the establishment of a republic and agitating for greater democracy and social reform.

Though from a poor working-class background, Houlding's family had attempted to run its own small business; they certainly could not be described as *petit-bourgeois*, but they were aspirational. John's parents were fond of talking of their 'Yeoman ancestry', and had attempted to hand their son the opportunity to attend an exclusive school. The Houldings were traditionalists, so the tumultuous events at home and abroad would have been defining for a young man with a conservative upbringing. He intended on fulfilling his parents' hopes of raising himself beyond his family's modest circumstances to make his fortune. For these reasons, John Houlding became diametrically opposed to radicalism in all its guises; opposed to anything that could subvert his own personal ambitions. The Conservative Party was, therefore, the natural home for John Houlding. It represented a bulwark against reformers and revolutionaries, and a bastion of traditionalism and stability. Houlding carried with him a lifetime of mistrust of both the Liberal Party, which he argued provided a political base for radicalism to agitate from, and any form of independent working-class politics, which would inevitably lead to the 'tyranny' of socialism.

Finally (and as much as these ideological attractions pulled Houlding towards the Conservative Party), Houlding had a very obvious material reason to call the Liverpool Conservative Party his home: his chosen profession as a brewer depended on that party's success. The Conservative Party in the city were dominated by brewers like Robert Cain and Andrew Barclay Walker, who had earned themselves the epithet from their enemies 'the beerocracy'. The Liverpool Conservative Party used their not inconsiderable influence to resist any legal restrictions magistrates may have sought to place on their trade—more especially on the number of public house licenses they issued.

HOULDING THE POLITICIAN

The inclusiveness of the Conservatives made them a welcoming home to aspiring working-class men like John Houlding. The Tory Party which Houlding committed to was the one led by the nineteenth-century political colossus, Benjamin Disraeli, and the Disraeli era was marked by a movement towards 'Tory Democracy'—the great cross-class political pact of the age. In essence, this was a pragmatic response to the passing of the 1867 Reform Act by the Liberal Government which had increased voting eligibility to include most industrial workers. Dealing with this new reality, the Conservatives were quick to realise (more so than their Liberal opponents) that if the nature of the electorate was changing, it would eventually bring about change in the type of candidate being elected. Recognition of this was manifest most obviously in their founding of the Working Men's Conservative Associations in the large towns and cities of Britain: 'Formed to spread Conservative principles among the masses of the people'.[7] It was an organisation keenly taken to in Liverpool. When John Houlding joined his local branch in Everton in 1868 there were twelve district branches in the city.[8] The Working Men's Conservative Association created a political cadre made up of skilled working-class men, small-business owners, and professionals who were wholeheartedly committed to the Tory cause. It was the perfect cross-class local organisation for Houlding to become involved with.

Houlding's natural flair for organisational management and his dominant personality virtually ensured that his membership of the Working Men's Conservative Association would be transformed into a desire to gain influence within it. Houlding made steady progress through its ranks, and by 1871 he was elected as chairman of the Everton Working Men's Conservative Association. This gave him command over the scores of members of the branch. His task as chairman was to organise the membership into an electoral machine capable of getting out the Conservative vote in force for all the elections taking place in the district, be they school board elections, municipal elections, or parliamentary elections. It also meant that Houlding, as branch chairman, was automatically entitled to become a member of the Constitutional Association, the ruling body of Liverpool Conservatism. This was a breakthrough moment, as it brought Houlding into contact for the first time with the party's civic elite.

Someone who had great influence upon Houlding's political development was Edward Whitley. Whitley was a solicitor but, like Houlding, he was connected to the brewing industry. As a member of a dynasty that controlled a much larger concern than Houlding's—the regional brewing giant, Greenall Whitley—Edward Whitley held great status among the so called 'beerocracy'. A town councilor for Everton from 1865, Whitley, though a product of the exclusive Rugby public school, had a popular touch and had immersed himself in the social life of the district with an uncommon gusto for the period, which set him apart from other, more aloof politicians. Whitley took part in church events, such as scriptural readings and tea parties, organised 'hot-pot' suppers (charity suppers to raise money for the poor), and became something of a philanthropist in the district by donating money for local projects.[9] This approach to maintaining his municipal seat and using it as a launch pad for higher office (Whitley became MP for Everton) was to be followed by Houlding. And it is almost certain that the patrician Whitley's control over Everton

taught Houlding one other valuable lesson: to secure the majority Protestant working-class vote of the district by joining their institutions. Effectively, this meant close association with, or membership of, the Orange
Order and a complete endorsement of their objective: the continuation of
Protestant ascendancy in Ireland, and that island's political union with
Britain. The script was written in Liverpool with little scope for devia-
tion: opposition to anything and anyone associated with the betterment of
the conditions of Roman Catholics or who advocated Irish independence.
That was the simple code that Liverpool Conservatism knew it had to
adopt, and it was a policy adhered to from top to bottom in the party.

There was much crossover in terms of ideology and personnel between the Working Men's Conservative Association, to which Houlding
already belonged, and the Orange Order. The Catholic-excluding Working Men's Conservative Association has been described by one commentator as 'the engine of Protestant power within the Conservative Party' in
Liverpool.[10] Whitley was careful to eulogise Orangemen, describing
them as 'model citizens' who were 'better educated' than any other body
of working men,[11] and so John Houlding too cultivated them by joining
'Kirkdale Glory Lodge'.[12] He also struck up a long-lasting friendship
with Thomas McCracken the Orange Order's Deputy Grandmaster in
Liverpool (an association, as we shall see, that opened up the opportunity
for McCracken to later involve himself with the hierarchy of Liverpool
FC).

On a side note: this connection Houlding had with the Orange Order—
and indeed the stronger one he had with the Working Men's Conservative
Association—has been a matter of some controversy (or, perhaps, the
cause of some embarrassment) for many Merseyside football commenta-
tors. Football clubs are today all-inclusive, nondiscriminatory organisations, so the whiff of exclusion, even from the dim and distant past, sits
uncomfortably with 'the brand' of the modern-day football club. This
connection, though, has to be seen in the context of the political environment at the time. Whether personally committed to a sectarian view or not
(and not being a diarist we have no access to Houlding's private thoughts
on the matter), to be Conservative and to hold ambitions for public office
at this point in the city's history required that one be fully committed to
Protestant-Unionism. That was just the reality of the situation.

Following in Whitley's footsteps, over the next decade John Houlding
consolidated his position in the north Liverpool political arena by impos-

ing his authority over grassroots Conservatism and assiduously building up his profile amongst the party leadership. As the chairman of a number of branches of the Working Men's Conservative Association in Everton and Kirkdale, Houlding had established an important fiefdom in north Liverpool and the efficient use he made of them helped determine the electoral fortunes of the party in the city as a whole. As the *de facto* leader of the Working Men's Conservative Association in the north end, Houlding was rewarded by being elected to the Everton Conservative Divisional Council (the district party's ruling body with powers over both municipal and parliamentary matters affecting Everton). And in 1884, he was elected as city councilor for Everton and Kirkdale ward, comfortably beating his Liberal opponent, David Hughes. The ward was far and away the largest in the city, with an electorate of twenty-one thousand voters—six to seven times the size of the average Liverpool council ward. It was a ward that held city-wide importance, and this was recognised by Houlding's elevation to the Constitutional Association's Executive Council: the ruling conclave of Liverpool Conservatism. As a local political figure, there were not too many men as powerful or as well known as John Houlding by the mid 1880s. He had also boosted his profile in Tory circles beyond the locality by befriending Viscount Sandon after his father the Earl of Harrowby, a former Liverpool MP, passed away in 1882. Houlding's rise may have been boosted by his networking of important people in the local party and beyond, but he gained traction with them only because he was a man of, and for, his time. He spoke with an authentic voice to the newly expanded electorate, now dominated by working men. And the party needed lieutenants like John Houlding.

Though the Conservative Party was in a seemingly impregnable position in Liverpool (it had been in continuous control of the council chamber from 1841), it was under increasing pressure in the last two decades of the nineteenth century by a resurgent Liberal Party. The Tory civic leadership were almost paranoid in their nightmare vision of a hostile triumvirate of trade unionists, temperance agitators, and those seeking Irish Home Rule—brought together and harnessed by a radicalised national Liberal Party under William Gladstone's leadership—taking their civic power away from them. In their artisan heartlands of Everton and its neighbouring district of West Derby, the challenge from one or more of these forces had materialised by the 1880s. Even in Everton, the jewel in the Tory crown, so called 'Lib-Lab' candidates (trade unionists standing as Liberal Party candidates) had taken to the field to test the Tories, hitherto almost unchallengeable in the district. And the drift of Roman Catholics into Everton had emboldened the Liberals to take more seriously the seemingly impossible task of unseating the Conservatives there. In the face of these developments, John Houlding became a critical figure in city politics. Indeed, this was a point of view held by Houlding himself. In 1883, he told a Working Men's Conservative Association meeting: 'If we once lose our hold of Everton, away would go our Conservative supremacy in Liverpool'.[13]

Houlding's flair for organisation and his combative style held the line for the Tories in Everton. Against the attack of an increasingly confident and militant temperance movement, Houlding appealed beyond them to the working class, countering their downbeat moral argument against 'the trade' by fiercely defending urban working-class leisure pursuits: an appeal to a 'democracy of drinkers'—positioning his political opponents as fanatics.[14] The political threat from organised labour was similarly repelled. Houlding's credentials as a former brewery drayman and also as leader of the Carters' Association (the most important workers' organisation in the district) allowed him a credible platform to position himself as the true representative of working-class interests. His strategy was to dismiss any Lib-Lab opponent as mere tools of radical Liberalism whose bidding they had been hoodwinked into doing. Alongside this, Houlding hammered home the traditional Tory message of continued resistance to the granting of Home Rule for Ireland—always a vote-winning argument amongst the Protestant working class.

Houlding was an important political figure for the Conservative Party and a man who was incredibly popular in his district. He had been elevated by Evertonians to the level of a monarch: 'King John of Everton'. Houlding was a man who projected the name of this mighty district far and wide, and fought the battles of his working-class base. They, in turn, gave him their political support. It came as no surprise then that his name was soon being talked of in terms of representing Everton at Westminster.

GUARDIAN AND OVERSEER

Away from politics, John Houlding was also involved in developing civil institutions in Everton during the 1870s and 1880s. The most influential

of these was the West Derby Union, a tier of the unfolding and burgeoning local state on Merseyside. Houlding joined the body in 1873 when he
was elected onto its board of guardians—essentially a governor for the
institution in the Everton area. By 1879 he had become chairman of the
whole organisation, a position he retained for the next two decades.

The logic of the poor law system was to avoid or minimise social
breakdown in large towns and cities, especially to prevent any law-and-
order problems arising from vagrancy. The West Derby Union, the
biggest poor law authority in the country, functioned by levying a rate at
parish level from local residents which would then be distributed to the
destitute as outdoor relief (a benefit often paid in return for work, but not
always). Rates would also be used to pay for the building and upkeep of
workhouses to accommodate the destitute, who would receive shelter and
food in return for work. Entry into the dreaded and foreboding workhouse
was viewed by those who populated them as a punishment as well as
relief. And they were meant to be punitive.

A report in the local press recounts a Boxing Day visit of John Houlding to a workhouse in Walton, a district in the north end of Liverpool.
'The inmates of the West Derby Union workhouse were supplied with the
customary dinner of roast beef, plum pudding, and one pint of beer for
those of the men who chose to take it. Mr John Houlding, the chairman of
the committee presented the inmates with oranges and apples, the old
men with tobacco and snuff, and the old women with an extra supply of
tea and sugar. Nearly 600 sat down to dinner, and the remaining 1,200,
mostly invalids, had their usual Christmas dinner supplied to them in their
wards'.[15] In the most unflattering of ways, this scene captures the famous
antiworkhouse ballad of the day: George Robert Sims' 'Christmas Day in
the Workhouse':

> It is Christmas Day in the workhouse,
> And the cold, bare walls are bright
> With garlands of green and holly,
> And the place is a pleasant sight;
> For with clean-washed hands and faces,
> In a long and hungry line
> The paupers sit at the table,
> For this is the hour they dine.
> And the guardians and their ladies,
> Although the wind is east,

Have come in their furs and wrappers,
To watch their charges feast;
To smile and be condescending,
Put pudding on pauper plates.
To be hosts at the workhouse banquet
They've paid for—with the rates.

Obviously, this is a perspective that hands us a harsh view of the motives of those overseeing the workhouse system and, in particular, any act of generosity they made. For many in north Liverpool who experienced the workhouse, the name of John Houlding would undoubtedly not have had pleasant associations, given that he was the man in ultimate charge of the workhouses there. From the vantage point of today, Houlding's position at the West Derby Union is not one that commands a lot of admiration. However, his connection with the administration of the dreaded work-houses of north Liverpool should be balanced in the context of his other extensive work on behalf of those left in penury. Houlding raised funds for the Seamen's Orphanage, the Retired Ex-Sailmakers Association, the Amalgamated Society of Railway Servants Orphanage Fund, and the Liverpool Operative Bakers and Confectioners Society pension fund. It would be harsh to dismiss him as the Victorian villain of the piece. In the milieu of his day, his charitable work (including the administration of the workhouses within the West Derby union's jurisdiction) would certainly have brought him approval amongst his peers.

The West Derby Union, though, did much more than carry out the poor law. It built and operated hospitals, convalescent homes, and or-phanages. The extensive nature of the larger poor law unions, such as the West Derby Union, is highlighted by the fact that in the biggest towns and cities of Britain they provided the physical and bureaucratic infra-structure of the British National Health Service and welfare state when those institutions were set up after the Second World War. For example, in Liverpool the city's existing Royal Liverpool Hospital, Walton Hospi-tal, and Alder Hey Children's Hospital were all founded by the West Derby Union as infirmaries in the late nineteenth century. From this it can be appreciated what a colossal responsibility John Houlding had as the man at the top of an organisation employing hundreds of men and women tasked with combating destitution and ill health across Liverpool and a large swathe of southwest Lancashire. Houlding's civic duties did not stop at involvement with the city council and the West Derby Union, though. In 1880, he also became the Overseer for the Township of Everton. As overseer, Houlding set the local rate to be levied and personally decided who were the deserving cases for cash donations.

The scope of Houlding's activities concerning welfare administration in late nineteenth-century Liverpool, therefore, was remarkable. Prior to the setting up of the National Health Service and the welfare state and the huge bureaucracies that accompanied them, an individual like John Houlding—if they had the energy and organisational abilities—could capture many influential positions in welfare organisations and build a considerable personal reputation in the sector.

It was for his work in the local state that Houlding was invited in May 1886 to a banquet held for Queen Victoria and her son, Prince Arthur, Duke of Connaught, at Liverpool Town Hall. The banquet was part of a three-day visit to Liverpool by the reigning monarch in celebration of her Golden Jubilee. The poor boy from Tenterden Street was now mixing in the rarefied company of royalty and the aristocracy. Along with other guests, John was given a memento of the occasion: a medal made of silver-gilt, composed of a wreath enclosing the figure of a Liverbird (the city's emblem) in enamel, overborn by a crown and engraved 'Visit of Her Majesty Queen Victoria to Liverpool, May 11th–13th, 1886'. For the record, the meal consisted of a starter of buttered sole fillets, a small course of lamb chops with rosemary and peas, a main course of pigeon cooked in red wine and served with asparagus in melted butter, and a dessert consisting of a selection of French pastries. This was a meal, it can be safely ventured, that would never be on the menu at the Walton workhouse.

A PATRON OF SPORT

Sport figured prominently in John Houlding's life, and he also used this to good effect in projecting himself in Everton. Houlding spoke publicly about the virtues of sport, not only for individual growth but for national survival and prosperity. 'It has been well said that the Battle of Waterloo was won on the cricket fields of England, because the game of cricket and other outdoor sports gave England the stamina to fight any opponents and to travel and colonise. I regard it as my duty to assist in the development of games which have helped to make England what she is today'.[16] Indeed, as a playing member of Breckfield Cricket Club, he presumably appreciated sport for its own intrinsic value too.

His colonial concerns aside, Houlding was a local populist politician, and by the end of the nineteenth century sport was certainly an activity that local political figures could earn status from. His initial involvement in sports patronage came in 1878 when he set up the Everton Quoits Club. The club's base was at Houlding's Cabbage Hall Inn on Breckfield Road, in the Anfield–Everton district. Quoits—a game involving the pitching from a distance of a metal or wooden ring in an attempt to land over a steel or wooden spike raised from the ground—was a popular game amongst the working classes in the north of England. The game in Liverpool was imported by migrants from Westmoreland and Cumberland who had come to seek work in the city. It was their 'northern rules' variety of quoits which prevailed. Usually played by teams of eight, there was indoor as well as outdoor quoits. Houlding took a firm grip of the club, becoming its first president, with his trusted brewery manager, John James Ramsey, installed as his vice president. Quoits was the first of many sports that would find its way into the portfolio of interests of John Houlding.

In the spacious grounds to the rear of the Sandon Hotel, meanwhile, Houlding played host to another newly formed sports outfit: the Everton Bowling Club. The club was established by locals in 1881 when housing development built over the common ground in Everton where both cricket and bowls used to be played and a green space was sought to ensure the club's continued existence. 'In this they were cordially met by Mr John Houlding', the *Liverpool Mercury* explained. 'At that time, Mr Houlding, in building the Sandon Hotel, secured a large plot at the back, which he has converted into an exceptional green. He has created a billiard pavilion and salon opening onto the ground, the design of which is on the continental plan'.[17] This was the type of press Houlding thrived on: projecting his sporting credentials and his image as local troubleshooter for community concerns. He had obviously put a lot of time and money into establishing the Sandon Hotel as a sports venue and recognition for it was pleasing. Attracting the bowlers to it would have done no harm either to the earnings of the Sandon. As with the quoits club, Houlding was made president of Everton Bowling Club, and John James Ramsey again joined him as his vice president, along with Alex Nisbet, a vaccination officer in his employ at the West Derby Union.

In the rest of the 1880s Houlding also found time to become president of the Everton Swimming Club, and to found a baseball club. In fact, Liverpool became something of a stronghold of baseball in England with its own league system, including (eventually) the playing of games at Anfield. Indeed, John Houlding went on to become president of the English Baseball Association. In 1886, the Liverpool Athletic News described Houlding as 'a staunch patron of sports'.[18] With his formal links to cricket, quoits, bowling, swimming, and baseball, it was a well-earned and appropriate accolade.

* * *

By the mid-1880s Houlding had constructed across Everton a network of influence in politics, the local state, and sports organisation. He had created an almost indispensable position for himself in the district where he increasingly resembled, not so much a prominent businessman-citizen, as a governor. Houlding had built his name in Everton by satisfying the yearning of a socially diverse population for identity, and by his undoubted (and conspicuous) commitment to invest his time and wealth in the district. In the 1880s, it was inconceivable for Houlding not to have placed his personal stamp of authority on any institution of note in the district. And so it proved with its most important institution of all: Everton Football Club, an organisation whose name would become known far and wide. If John Houlding's star was a fast-rising one in late nineteenth-century Liverpool, his connection to the city's preeminent sporting club would accelerate its ascendancy.

3

FROM HERO TO VILLAIN

John Houlding was at the vanguard of establishing sports clubs in Everton, but the one major sporting institution in the district which eclipsed all others was created without any input from him. Everton Football Club had been in existence as a district outfit since 1879, two years before Houlding became involved with the club in 1881. By that time the club had its own playing area and had gained a reputation as the premier football team in the city. As John Houlding could view from the rear of his own home, Stanley House, which almost backed onto the pitch Everton FC had claimed on Stanley Park, the young club were already attracting hundreds of spectators to its games.

This was uncharacteristic tardiness on Houlding's part; as an organisation with stature operating in the district, one might have expected him to have the matter in hand. This apparent sluggishness is not without explanation, though. First of all, Everton FC had its roots in the church and chapel football teams that came into existence in the rapidly urbanising district of Everton during the 1870s. Local teams, such as the team from the Sunday school of the New Connexional Methodist chapel, St Domingo, and Church of England teams like St Peter's, St Benedicts, and St Mary's, were founded by evangelical Christians ministering to urban communities—so called 'muscular Christians'. Their prime aim was to keep young men from frequenting public houses and gambling, and to embrace a life of temperance. One influential figure in the embryonic Everton was the Yorkshire-born Reverend Ben Chambers, the minister at St Domingo New Connexional Methodist Chapel. The evangelising

Chambers arrived in Liverpool in June of 1877 determined to improve the lot of his new congregation and was quickly into his stride in setting up his new chapel's Band of Hope temperance group. A year later Chambers set up first a cricket team, and then a football team.

Quite obviously, then, the culture that gave rise to the embryonic Everton FC would have been hostile to a man like Houlding and all that he represented. Second, the decision made by Liverpool Corporation at the end of the 1870s to make its parkland available for use to the general public for recreation purposes had provided playing space for a host of football teams. Hitherto, the parks were only accessible to the residents of the well-to-do homeowners whose houses abutted them—like John Houlding, for example. The decision to throw open the gates of the city's parks ensured that Everton not only had a pitch to play their matches on, but also easy access to an abundance of teams to test themselves against and to hone their competitive skills. John Houlding at this early stage of the club's history had virtually nothing to offer the emerging team. Eventually, however, Everton FC did require his support.

As the club sought to expand their horizons beyond being the undisputed kings of Stanley Park and establish themselves on a region-wide basis, they required a headquarters and a secretary to administrate the club. Offering his services at this point was not John Houlding, however, but local publican—and another Tory councilor for the district of Everton—John W. Clarke. Clarke stole a march on Houlding by offering his Queens Head Hotel as a club HQ and himself as club secretary. Clarke was a genial man and enthusiastic about sports; a member of Stanley Cricket Club, whose players are said by the earliest historians of Everton FC to have been the team's most vocal supporters in their time on the pitches of Stanley Park.[1] Perhaps Clarke's early support for the team made it more palatable for the club's players to set aside whatever reservations they might have had of taking up a publican's offer? By this stage, though, it is likely that the young Christian evangelists who had initiated church and chapel football teams could not exercise control over the identity of their outgrowth—being moved about from diocese to diocese on a regular basis perhaps contributed to this loss of control. The Reverend Ben Chambers, for one, left St Domingo around the same time as the Everton club's headquartering at a public house. In any event, the players and coaches were comfortable with using Clarke. He became not only Everton secretary but also its treasurer, and he appears to have had a flair for organising the fledgling club with fixtures against the very best teams that Liverpool and the rest of Lancashire had to offer. By 1882, however, and for reasons that are unclear, Clarke had to leave Liverpool. At that point, the administration of the club was left to Clarke's deputy, Tom Evans, another Stanley Cricket Club member and former Everton FC player. The club had their new secretary, but finding new headquarters was a separate matter. Step forward John Houlding. His opportunity had come around, and he was ready for it.

PRESIDENT AND LANDLORD

In fact, Houlding had already begun to take up a closer relationship with the club prior to this point, having become a club member in late 1881. Clarke's departure months later was the moment Houlding was waiting for. The acceptance of his offer to use the Sandon Hotel as club HQ brought him the club presidency. Quite obviously this was a step up and away from Houlding's other sporting associations in terms of scale. Everton FC were a burgeoning organisation with the unmistakable potential for mass appeal. Its possibilities in terms of status and political influence were obvious, and so too was the scope for financial reward. Entrepreneurs in Liverpool were increasingly looking to capitalise on the public's interest in sports by investing their money to enclose land, erect grandstand facilities, and provide a sporting spectacle for their customers. By the 1870s Liverpool already had a tradition of commercialised sports. Strawberry Gardens near Everton was the site of athletic meetings that drew thousands of paying spectators to watch famous athletes from around the country. In the north of the city, two companies were formed, the Stanley Athletic Grounds Company and the Liverpool Athletics Grounds Company, in order to tap into the demand for track and field events. And a local gate-taking cricket league was set up in the 1880s. As a businessman looking to profit, John Houlding would not be left behind in the race to secure some of this action. Houlding's association with the club would last a decade and the club in that time would rise to national prominence. However, his relationship with it was always an uneasy one, and the nature of Houlding's core business, and his sharp commercial practices were the reasons for this unease. There is a clear sense that he was an interloper; he and Everton FC were ill matched from the outset. The reckoning for that difficult relationship, though, was for the future.

President or not, in 1882 Houlding's path to control at Everton was not yet cleared. His introduction to the Everton setup came at a time when the club committee were perhaps looking beyond him to land a bigger fish. The Everton Committee had made an appeal in the Liverpool press for the 'gentlemen of the city' to support the club:

> Allow us to introduce to your notice the position attained by the above-named organisation [Everton] and to solicit your most valued sympathy and support. Established in 1879, it has gradually improved in strength and importance, until it now occupies a position second to none in the district; nor do its claims to consideration rest here, for as the club has, season by season, grown in strength, its effect upon the public has been both marked and encouraging, so much so, that at any of its important fixtures there are large gatherings of persons, numbering 1,500 to 2,000, seeking the Saturday afternoon's recreation, which the public parks are intended to provide for. In order to popularise the game, we are this year [1882] playing a number of clubs of considerable renown from long distances.[2]

This appeal was meant to attract the attention of local political and business figures, and some responded to the call by becoming members of the club. David MacIver, the cofounder of the Cunard Shipping Line and the Conservative MP for Birkenhead, and Lord Sandon, a Liverpool Conservative MP, allowed their names to be used as patrons of the club; another local notable respondee to the Everton Committee's call was James Barkeley-Smith, vice chairman of the Liverpool Chamber of Commerce and a director of the Liverpool United Gas Company. The appeal's success in 'snaring' such eminent men must have elicited both excitement and trepidation for Houlding at this point. Excitement in the sense that many well-known Tory politicians and businessmen were now members of an organisation he was already a prominent figure within; trepidation because these men were richer and better known than he, and they could possibly by taking up leading roles in the club eclipse him. In the event, though, these new high-profile members of Everton FC chose to take only an honorary role in the club, and Houlding was left with a free run to consolidate his position and strengthen it with financial investment.

Prior to Houlding's input, the club committee had tried financing the club via membership fees. Everton needed to pay its expenses: payment to players (on an informal basis—professionalism not being legitimate until 1885); train fares to and from away games in the northwest of England; and for basic costs, such as uniforms, boots, nets, and balls. A club membership annual subscription was levied, but that nowhere near covered the club's outgoings. As a member of the Lancashire Football Association and attracting to Liverpool dominant Lancastrian clubs like Preston North End, Bolton Wanderers, and Blackburn Rovers, Everton had established itself as the city's strongest and most appealing team to support. Its weekly fixtures were attracting thousands of spectators—however, they were nonpaying spectators. This needed to change, urgently. Cash from gate receipts would give the club a fighting chance of maintaining its best players, attracting others, and paying for club expenses. In 1883, in preparation for the 1883–1884 season, a plan was hatched to vacate Stanley Park and to hire a field, not far away at Priory Road, from a local farmer: a Mr William Cruitt. The club railed off a playing pitch, and a local builder was employed to erect crude terracing in order to charge spectators a fee to watch Everton's games. The Cruitt field experiment, though, was short lived. The club took just fourteen shillings for the gate from their first game of the 1883/84 season, and £50 for the season as a whole. On top of this, Cruitt refused to agree an extension to the club to use his field for the following season on the not entirely unreasonable grounds that the football crowds disturbed the peace of the neigbourhood—though this is something he might have been able to anticipate in advance of his initial agreement with the committee. The reality was, though, that at the end of the 1883–1884 season the Everton Committee were left with the dilemma of finding a new home ground. Without a permanently secured, well-constructed home ground, their club of five years standing faced an uncertain future. The club looked to John Houlding, their president, for assistance.

Houlding's grip on Everton FC began in earnest at this vulnerable point for the club. His suggested solution to the ground problem was to take up residence on a plot of land (eventually called Anfield) which was owned by fellow brewer and acquaintance, Joseph Orrell. Orrell, however, had a proviso: he would lease his land only to Houlding, as only he could guarantee that a regular annual rental would be paid—perhaps a fair position to take given the club's own parlous financial situation. Any such move to Anfield would have the added bonus for Houlding of the club's ground being close to his Sandon Hotel—a long stone's throw away. For the Everton Committee, which had been facing the prospect of playing the new league season back on open parkland, the Houlding-Orrell offer was a welcome lifeline; not only did the club have the prospect of secure tenure for seasons to come, it would be Houlding taking the ultimate risk on financing the new ground.

The only fly in the ointment was that the land was owned by Joseph Orrell to be leased out to the club, and uncertainty prevailed given that an outsider could at some stage—as Cruitt had done—refuse to renew the lease for the land, undermining any prospect of physically building a stable future there. This, though, seemed settled when, in 1885, Orrell placed his land up for sale. Speaking to a local weekly sporting newspaper in 1887, the club secretary, Alex Nisbet, explained the process leading to Everton FC laying down firm foundations for their future at Anfield:

> After a couple of seasons the then owner [Joseph Orrell] was about to sell the field for building purposes, and knowing that there was not another site to be had in the neighbourhood, a deputation was appointed to wait on Mr John Houlding, well aware of the interest which he takes in all kinds of sport indulged in by our working men. Our difficulties were placed before him, his support was solicited, and advice asked as to what could be done. Now what he did, in answer to our appeal, was this. He bought the ground and let it to the club at a rental which only amounts to one and a quarter per cent on the outlay.[3]

It has to be said, Nisbet's words place Houlding in a slightly flattering light as savior (Nisbet was in the employ of Houlding at the West Derby Union and so his recollection of events need to be viewed in that context), but his framing of Houlding's intervention as crucial *is* justified.

Houlding was now, effectively, Everton's landlord as well as its president. It had taken him four years of assiduous cultivation, but now he could take the club more firmly into his growing portfolio of interests and begin to reap the benefits. Indeed, his association with the club had already proven to be beneficial: Houlding's securing of a seat in the council chamber in 1884 was a victory in no small measure aided by the players and members of Everton FC who had canvassed for votes in the district on their president's behalf.[4] Political capital was important to John

Houlding. So too was turning a profit. That was a lesson the committee-men at Everton would eventually learn.

With a rich man at its helm, the conditions were established for the club to attempt to satisfy its ambitions. With John Houlding's cash backing them, Everton had the wherewithal to do what its Lancashire rivals were able to do: employ top professional players. Everton raided Kilmarnock FC in Scotland and took back with them to Liverpool Alec Dick and his fellow Scot, George Fleming. Welshman George Farmer was also signed from Oswestry Town. Joining them were English professionals George Dobson and Bob Smalley, signed from Bolton Wanderers and Preston North End, respectively. These additions, however, did not in the short term provide Everton with the level of success they craved. It remained the case, certainly, that locally they were almost beyond dispute the dominant club. The litmus test for that was the Liverpool Senior Cup, which in Houlding's time at Everton the club won six times. However, against their mighty northwest of England rivals they still struggled to be seen as worthy opponents. For example, Everton were denied entry into the Lancashire Senior Cup, the Lancashire Football Association's premier competition. The Senior Cup was competed for between luminaries of the county's football scene like Bolton Wanderers, Burnley, Preston North End, and Blackburn Rovers. Instead, Everton were invited to play in the Lancashire Junior Cup, along with minnow clubs such as Southport and Blackpool. It was a hugely frustrating time for the ambitious Liverpool club.

One thing Everton were excelling at, though, was attracting regular first-class opposition to Anfield for exhibition games. Under Houlding, Everton had increased its stadium capacity and upgraded facilities for players and supporters alike. Although keeping the ambitious Everton at arm's length in terms of admission to the Lancashire Senior football scene, the clubs of the Lancastrian elite were keen on visiting Anfield to play. And the best teams the Midlands had to offer, such as Derby County, Aston Villa, Wolverhampton Wanderers, and West Bromwich Albion, were regular visitors to the north end of Liverpool, too. Even teams from Scotland, like Partick Thistle, Glasgow Rangers, and Glasgow Celtic, made the long journey south of the border to play Everton.

All of these clubs were attracted by the developing stadium's atmosphere and, of course, a share of the gate receipts from the large attendances they helped attract. Houlding had taken Anfield from the eight thousand to ten thousand capacity the club were restricted to when first taking up tenancy on Orrell's land to a twenty-thousand-capacity, purpose-built stadium by 1887. The ground at this point had two covered grandstands and steep, banked enclosures behind each goal—the Oakfield Road end enclosure being the basis for what eventually became 'the Kop', the renowned 'home end' of the stadium where the most fanatical of supporters stood. In the wake of these improvements, gate receipts rocketed from the £200 taken in the club's inaugural season at Anfield in 1884–1885, to almost £1,500 for the 1887–1888 season. It was a stadium that commanded attention, and it would soon be hosting games in the inaugural season of the English Football League when Everton, against all expectations, became one of its twelve founding members.

How could this have come to pass? How could a club thought not good enough to compete in Lancashire's premier cup competition have been chosen to kick off the English Football League's maiden season along with eleven of the country's top clubs? The answer is two-fold: the commercial pragmatism of the Football League, and the persuasive powers of John Houlding. As mentioned, Everton's status in the game outside of Liverpool was not recognised, and the architect of the Football League, Aston Villa president William McGregor, did not have Everton in mind or on his mailing list when he notified a number of his fellow club presidents in March 1887 of his intention to set up a national league—an idea that had been discussed in football circles for a year or two before finally happening. A provisional list of the clubs chosen to play in the new national league confirmed that, as expected, Everton were out in the cold. A determined Houlding, though, had other ideas. He set his attention on courting the then two most prestigious clubs in the country, Aston Villa and Preston North End, in an effort to make the final list of clubs. The Aston Villa president, William McGregor, and William Sudell, the Preston president, were considered to be the most powerful men in football. In the wake of Everton's name not making the provisional league list, Houlding had his club secretary, Alex Nisbet, invite both Aston Villa and Preston to play at Anfield. The approach to Aston Villa proved decisive. The Birmingham club played Everton at Anfield in April 1887 and McGregor was mightily impressed by the surroundings, telling his Everton counterpart his club's amenities were advanced and agreeable. Soon after, the Aston Villa secretary arranged a return fixture between the two clubs at their own Wellington Road stadium in Birmingham; the Aston

Villa secretary commenting, 'We have visited your ground and you have never been here, there is no doubt you would be a considerable draw. Will you, therefore, play here. I feel sure it would pay you well'.[5]

Houlding's nudge had paid off handsomely. Less than three weeks after being left off McGregor's shortlist, Everton were notified that they were indeed to be one of the twelve founding members of the Football League. McGregor later admitted that many of the better teams in England had been rejected in favour of Everton whose attendances could help make the venture a financial success. Regardless of *Realpolitik*, though, this was an astonishing coup for Houlding given that, comfortably, Everton had a far inferior competitive record than a host of better-known football clubs in the country, including such established outfits such as Nottingham Forest and Sheffield Wednesday. Even locally on Merseyside, nearby Bootle FC could make a case for having as much grounds for consideration of a place in the Football League as Everton, given that they held an impressive competitive record against the best teams in the game and that their Hawthorne Road ground was of a very decent standard and capacity. No matter, Everton were in the Football League and primed to become one of England's premier clubs.

HAIL THE CONQUERING HERO

This huge competitive step up, however, was daunting. It necessitated the spending of much more money on players if the club were to seize its opportunity. This, as usual, meant the spending of John Houlding's money. With Everton now competing in the Football League, top professionals were only too willing to join the club. England internationals Johnny Holt and Edgar Chadwick transferred from Bootle and Blackburn Rovers, respectively. Scottish internationals Nick Ross and Bob Kelso joined the club from Preston North End. Houlding's cash was being used to poach players from some of the best teams in the country. One thousand pounds was also spent on more stadium improvements to make spectators more comfortable. Preceding these alterations there was a disagreement between Houlding and the club committee over the wisdom of carrying out the work so close to the Football League season's start, but the club president had his way. As well as improving the stadium, a number of additional turnstiles were included around the ground in anticipation of higher gates. This proved to be a wise decision. In the recent past, only games against local arch rivals Bootle FC had been a fixture that could test the capacity of Anfield. The opening league season, though, saw regular attendances of between eight thousand to ten thousand, with soon-to-be crowned league champions Preston North End attracting a hefty fifteen thousand to Anfield. In subsequent seasons Anfield could barely contain the massive attendances Everton were attracting. The surge in match-day numbers forced John Houlding on one occasion to warn attendees of the possible dangers from gangs of pickpockets, attracted to the area because of the bustling crowds milling about the stadium. Houlding instructed the club secretary to 'get notices printed to be posted at pay gates informing "Beware Pickpockets"'.[6] Houlding's undoubtable public spiritedness also had the happy byproduct of keeping gate money out of the hands of thieves and in the club's hands.

In the league's first season, Everton finished a creditable eighth, higher placed than much-fancied clubs like Stoke City and Burnley. During the season Everton also beat top outfits like Aston Villa, Blackburn Rovers, and Bolton Wanderers. Not bad for a club many considered unfit to contend with the very best that Lancashire had to offer. However, matters were to get considerably better after Everton signed attacker Fred Geary from Notts Rangers in 1889. One of seven new recruits to the first team group that summer, Geary would be described in today's football parlance as 'a goal machine'. In the young Englishman's first season he scored twenty-one goals in twenty-two games, catapulting Everton to the runners-up spot behind an all-powerful Preston North End team who had retained their crown (the famous 'Invincibles' team). Increased investment in playing staff had been justified and the team were going from strength to strength. In the following season, 1890–1891, Geary continued his marksmanship with a twenty-goal haul and Everton went one place better to become champions of England.

It had been a meteoric rise for the club: in the space of ten years it had been transformed from a district team, battling it out for local park supremacy with scores of other hopeful clubs, to the greatest team in England. It was an achievement that John Houlding would not fail to exploit. It was his money that had transformed the fortunes of the club, and he knew it. In the days succeeding the club's triumph, Houlding called for a public celebration of the achievement. These were the days before a victorious team would tour its hometown, displaying their trophy in open top buses, so there would not be that scale of recognition. However, a large audience packed into the auditorium of Liverpool College on the evening of 8 May 1891 to see the formal presentation of the Football League trophy to the club. The choice of venue was a significant one for Houlding. As an Old Lerpoolian, Houlding had returned to his *alma mater* bringing with him the League Championship trophy—apart from the FA Cup the most important trophy in football.

The great and the good of the city were assembled to bear witness to Everton's momentous success. These were the moments John Houlding had dreamt of and worked so hard to make a reality, and this night was a chance to gather salutations from the social elite. Houlding rose to his feet and, after acknowledging the time and effort of the audience to attend the occasion, accepted the trophy on behalf of the newly crowned Football League champions. 'We have seen some of the most brilliant victories that have been celebrated in this country. We have now won, and deservedly, one of the finest cups in Great Britain. It is our duty to do all in our power to keep possession of the cup'.[7] The night of celebration at the Collegiate was brought to a close with the singing of Georg Friedrich Handel's 'See the Conquering Hero Comes'. As he surveyed the scene of the football triumph, Houlding had every right to be a satisfied man. As the valedictory song rang out in the hall of his old college he could have been forgiven for thinking its refrain related to him as much as the football victors:

> See the conquering hero comes!
> Sound the trumpets, beat the drums.
> Sports prepare, the laurel bring,
> Songs of triumphs to him sing.

Houlding was nearing the peak of his power and influence. His control of the city's football club—now the foremost sporting club in the country—gave him huge civic profile. The local press ensured this by giving even more attention to the exploits of the 'winter game' in Liverpool. As someone who stood at the brink of selection for parliamentary honours, he had done his chances no harm by bringing great sporting honour to the city. Indeed, it was probably the case that John Houlding's association with Everton FC was as much of an identifier for him with the general public as his central role in the administration of the city. Combined, they made the name 'Houlding' one of the most recognisable in Liverpool, and his actions were closely followed and commented upon in the daily newspapers and society journals. His words and deeds carried weight.

If his public life was in fine fettle, so too was his private life. Houlding, like any Victorian man of means, was keen to see his children progress up the social scale; with daughters expected to 'marry well' and an anticipation that sons would strike out into careers with status. Daughter Alice-Margaret and son William did not fail their father's expectations. In 1888, Alice-Margaret Houlding married Thomas Knowles, a scion of the wealthy Knowles family of Wigan in Lancashire. The Knowles held significant interests in coal mines and in brewing. No doubt John Houlding would have been particularly pleased that Thomas Knowles was a solid, true-blue Conservative, and, like him, a member of the ruling body of Liverpool Conservatism: the Constitutional Association. In fact, his son-in-law was the nephew of the Conservative Member of Parliament for Wigan between 1874 and 1883: his namesake, Thomas Knowles. Alice-Margaret and Thomas's union produced two grandsons for John and wife Jane: Thomas Henry Knowles and William Dowdney Knowles.

Houlding's son, William, was also in the ascendant and would further have buoyed John's mood. William at first enrolled at University College Liverpool (the precursor to the University of Liverpool) and qualified there as a barrister. Deciding this not to be his forte, however, he turned towards studying industrial chemistry and graduated from Edinburgh University with a science degree. The switch was almost certainly with a mind to joining his father in his brewing business—a knowledge of chemistry being a necessity to keep abreast of industry techniques. After graduating from Edinburgh University, William joined his father and brewery manager, John James Ramsey, in the day-to-day running of Houlding's Sparkling Ales. William had also become involved with Conservative politics in the city. He was in regular attendance at the various Working Men's Conservative Association meetings in Liverpool's north end and a member of more than one branch. It seems clear that his father, John, was a major influence on William.

All in all, in the summer of 1891, with his football team riding high and his own public and private life in good order, John Houlding must have been a contented figure—his continued success apparently an inevitability. Storm clouds were gathering though, and any hubris Houlding might have had was to be punished. Only months after the triumphant return to Liverpool College with his championship-winning Everton team, he faced a series of struggles in the football club which would eventually envelop the rest of his public life. For the first time in his career John Houlding's credibility would be tested and questioned. The forward march of Houlding was about to be halted.

FACTIONALISM AT EVERTON FC

In truth, the portents were already there at Everton FC, as the club's governance had for a long time been beset by factionalism. Although it was widely accepted by both insiders and outsiders to the club that Houlding and his money had been instrumental in the development of Everton, hostility to the president grew amongst the membership when, towards the end of the 1880s, he began to insist on remuneration for the financial commitments he had made. This, principally, related to Houlding's demand for the full rate of interest agreed with the Everton Committee on money he had paid out for the club's Anfield Road ground improvements. Rather than a beneficent patron of the club, the president was increasingly viewed by sections of its membership as a rentier with self-interest uppermost in mind.

For all of Houlding's financial commitment to Everton, control of the club still rested formally with the club's committee. The committee consisted of Houlding as president, one vice president of the club, a treasurer and assistant treasurer, secretary and assistant secretary, and seven ordinary members of the club. They enjoyed as a body 'absolute control of the ground and finances, the arrangement of matches and selection of teams and other matters affecting the interests of the club'.[8] It would appear, therefore, that Houlding's ability to determine the destiny of Everton in an autocratic manner was limited. However, as president, he could elevate to the committee one club member to supplement the officers of the club, many of whom were business or political associates of his and who appear to have faced little opposition in gaining their positions. The list of officers of the club from the mid 1880s through to the split in 1892 reveals a cluster of Houlding loyalists, men who would later side with the president in the club split and help to set up Liverpool Football Club thereafter.[9] Houlding, therefore, was well placed to have a great say over club governance. This state of affairs, however, relied on the passivity of the club's large membership, and matters were about to change on that score.

Membership figures for the club in its formative period are not publicly recorded prior to the press coverage of the growing factionalism in 1891 and 1892. In October of 1891, Houlding is quoted as totaling the club membership at approximately five hundred (three hundred of whom, he declared with obvious irritability, were 'practically new to the club').[10] The extent of this influx of members is corroborated by the club minutes, which show a marked rise in membership from 1889.[11] We can take it, therefore, that during the bulk of the 1880s club membership stood at, or near, two hundred. The membership voted annually to choose committee members. A democratic system of one person, one vote prevailed. However, the local press detected that 'caucuses' and 'cliques'—for the purpose of electing to the committee groups of individuals with common goals and grievances—was a feature of club affairs, and this could have gone some way to compromising the one-person–one-vote code.[12] This may have been the means by which Houlding consolidated his power at the club. It appears, though, that as the club membership became ever larger it was increasingly difficult for the president and his supporters to retain control of the situation, and, as a result, the voices of those opposing Houlding grew louder and his detractors became more organised and determined to see a change of order at the top of the club.

The first time it became apparent that relations within the hierarchy of the club were not harmonious was in the summer of 1888. With gate receipts increasing considerably, Houlding began to receive more rental money from the club for the use of Anfield. Houlding was entitled under the terms of an earlier agreement with the club committee to charge the club £250 per annum. This figure was roughly equal to 4 per cent on the £6,000 Houlding had paid to Joseph Orrell in 1885 for the land on which the club ground stood. The club had previously paid Houlding £100 per season; roughly 1.5 per cent on Houlding's £6,000 outlay. At the 1888 Annual General Meeting it was agreed to pay Houlding £150 for the coming season's rental payment. But the sensitivity over the issue of the club's rental charge can be gleaned by the (still-Houlding-controlled) committee's rebuttal of a local press story claiming the club were now already paying Houlding £200 per annum.[13]

Houlding's refusal to commit himself to a long-term lease for Everton to rent his land (the club committee negotiated annually with Houlding) unnerved the Everton membership, bringing about a decision by the committee—no doubt a reluctantly taken one, given the men loyal to Houlding serving on it—to block any further loans from the president until the matter of tenancy was resolved.[14] Houlding had previously charged the club 5 per cent interest on money loaned for stadium improvements and for the purchase of professional players. However, the committee's resolve faltered only months later. In November 1888, seeking to cash in on the unexpectedly large response of the public to their matches in the inaugural season of the Football League, the committee took out another loan of £1,000 from Houlding.[15] It was clear from these events that if the disquiet amongst the membership over the direction of the club were to be taken seriously then a new body of men on the committee would be required.

In the run-up to the following year's Annual General Meeting in 1889, the local press reported on a number of meetings amongst certain members of the club who were intent on unseating those on the committee they felt were unwilling to steer the club away from its apparent course of passivity toward, or even collusion with, John Houlding. In May 1889, the Liverpool Review carried a report on Everton members who were 'determined to oust the present executive and replace it by one of their own'. 'The clique', as the *Liverpool Review* named them, accused the serving officers of the club of 'laxity' in their financial management of it. The so-called clique's solution was to propose a raft of members of the club whom they 'were prepared to elect at all costs'.[16]

A week later, those loyal to Houlding within the club held their own meeting, denouncing the rebels' stance and agreeing a strategy to put forward their own candidates for the committee elections. The Houlding loyalists proposed the reelection of the bulk of the sitting committee to maintain the status quo in the president's favour.[17]

The club's 1889 Annual General Meeting was eagerly awaited. When it sat, Houlding's detractors provoked a heated debate over club finances; bringing up the issue of club money having been spent on a building contract for the stadium without either first being agreed to by the club committee, or even being put out for competitive tender. Criticism was also levelled at the club treasurer for running up expenses (unspecified) that were not agreed to by the committee. These criticisms were defended by Houlding himself, who was also forced by the floor of the meeting to explain the hike in rental costs the club had faced in the previous year, and which it would continue to face in the upcoming year (the cost of renting Houlding's land had risen from £100 for the season of 1887–1888, to £240 for the season of 1888–1889, and then to £250 for the season of 1889–1890).[18] Despite this opposition, Houlding was able to persuade the membership to reelect a key ally, the sitting secretary, William E. Barclay. Barclay had seniority and a powerful voice amongst the membership—he was a man who would later become the first secretary of Houlding's new Liverpool FC. Matters were too heated, however, to agree on the election of the rest of the committee for the coming season and the issue was deferred to a later date.

It would appear that this strategy took the wind out of the sails of those members seeking wholesale changes to tether Houlding. When the committee was eventually selected, six of the thirteen-man committee were incumbent members of it (with five other members not having had to stand for reelection). However, two men who did make it onto the committee were Abraham Thomas Coates and William Robert Clayton. Their presence must be viewed as an advance party that heralded the arrival onto the Everton Committee of a new generation of men—ones who were unimpressed by the personal history of key figures in the development of the organisation (nor, indeed, the president's politics and the use he made of the club to advance them).

As the next two seasons unfolded, culminating in the crowning of Everton as English champions in 1891, the outstanding issue of the club's security of tenure at Anfield became an ever more pressing matter. At the same time, with more astute planning for elections by 'the clique', newer club members took up their positions within the committee room and posed a greater challenge each year to the old guard within it who had built up a working relationship with John Houlding. The tide had at last begun to turn against Houlding. In 1890, Dr James Clement Baxter, a newcomer to the club in 1889, joined the reelected Abraham Coates and William Clayton on the committee. And at the following year's Annual General Meeting, James Griffiths, John Atkinson, and Francis Currier, also later arrivals as club members in 1889, joined Baxter, Clayton, and Coates on the committee. All six men would go on to become original directors of the newly formed Everton Football Club Limited Company in 1892. By this point, then, Houlding could definitely rely only on his stalwarts William E. Barclay, Thomas Howarth, John James Ramsey, and Alex Nesbit for support in the club committee.[19] The nonaligned members of that body—William Jackson, Richard Molyneux, and Richard Stockton—held the balance of power.

THE 1891 LIMITED LIABILITY COMPANY SCHEME

The club was again thrown into turmoil with the emerging news in the autumn of 1891 that Joseph Orrell had invoked a clause in the contract signed by Houlding in 1885 when buying his land. Joseph Orrell sold the land to Houlding prior to departing to another part of the country with his family, with the stipulation that the perimeter of the land belonging to his uncle, a Mr. John Orrell, which abutted the Anfield Road ground, must remain undisturbed. If at any point John Orrell decided to prepare his adjoining land for building purposes, then Houlding would be obliged to join with him in laying an access road between their properties. This was an understandable clause to insert into the sale as the last two decades of the nineteenth century saw a boom in private housebuilding in the suburban districts of Liverpool. However, the clause, when invoked and acted upon, would have disturbed the covered standing enclosures that had been erected on the 'Orrell side' of the club's ground and, bound by thoroughfares on its other perimeters, preventing a remodeling of the stadium, would have necessitated removal from the ground by the club. It is clear from press coverage of the affair that the Everton membership had long been aware of this 'Sword of Damocles' hanging over the future of the club's home ground. When in August of 1891 John Orrell instructed his uncle to invoke the clause agreed between him and Houlding, enmity was expressed towards him from Houlding's supporters and opponents alike, believing that John Orrell had bided his time on this issue.

Regardless of the unanimity on who was to blame for the predicament, however, the 'Orrell complication' provided the battleground for another war of words between Houlding and his supporters and the caucus within the membership who had now rallied around the triumvirate of William Clayton and Dr James Clement Baxter, sitting committee members, and George Mahon, a prominent member of the club.

Houlding's opponents believed that, as landlord, the club president should negotiate with Orrell and pay him an agreeable rent for his land in order to retain continued tenancy. For his part, Houlding saw the way forward through the club's purchase of both his and Orrell's properties via the club's formation into a limited company. The core of Houlding's proposal was to sell his land to the proposed new company at the land value he had paid for it in 1884, £6,000. John Orrell's land would be bought by the company for slightly less than £5,000. From Houlding's stated perspective, his proposed scheme would secure the club's location, allow the club to expand the stadium and increase ground capacity, and afford the possibility of creating an athletics track which could maximise stadium utility during the close season. From the perspective of his critics in the club, his proposals amounted to an exploitation of Everton's difficulties with Orrell in order to gain total control of the club via a limited liability scheme where he would dominate the shareholding. The opposition of the membership to Houlding was organised and implacable from this point on. The committee were now resolved to leaving Anfield behind, and Houlding with it, to set up a stadium elsewhere.

* * *

Barely six months after the greatest achievement of Houlding's public life—standing at the head of a sports organisation that had bestowed great prestige on his native city and which greatly elevated his own personal status—he was now threatened with the loss of this important social asset. The scene was set for a final reckoning for John Houlding at Everton FC. However, Houlding was not just facing troubles within the totemic football club. By late 1891 he was also facing a challenge to his political powerbase, as emerging social forces within the north end of Liverpool threatened his, and the Tory Party's, rule there.

Liverpool College, 'the Collegiate', Shaw Street, Liverpool. This building is the surviving piece of the college John Houlding attended in the mid-1840s.

Fazakerley Cottage Homes for children, built by the West Derby Union in 1889 and pioneered by John Houlding. The tree-lined avenue has twenty-four large cottages; the large building with the tower was the central assembly hall. The site also contained schools, a workshop, infirmary, and swimming baths.

The customs house on Liverpool's waterfront. As a young man, Houlding was employed there as a messenger. *Heritage Image Partnership Ltd/Alamy stock photo.*

Houlding's influence over the Working Men's Conservative Association in the north end of Liverpool allowed him a platform to ascend the ranks of the Liverpool Conservative Party. *Keith Morris/Alamy stock photo.*

Front of Stanley House (on Anfield Road, twenty yards from the present stadium), the mansion built for John Houlding and his family in 1876. Houlding lived there until his death in 1902.

Rear of Stanley House, which abuts Stanley Park.

The Sandon Hotel, Anfield. John Houlding's public house was headquarters first to Everton FC and then Liverpool FC. The original tiled frontage has recently been covered.

The main building of the Walton Workhouse site, now part of the Mersey Care NHS Trust. Built in 1864, it accommodated over two thousand inmates. John Houlding was chairman of the West Derby Union, which governed the institution.

The Cabbage Hall public house. Owned by John Houlding, it was here in 1879 that he began his experimentation with sports entrepreneurship by hosting the Everton Quoits Club.

Stanley Park, the parkland where football in the city of Liverpool was established.

Entrance to Stanley Park. The car park is directly behind John Houlding's Stanley House home and was the original site of the pitch that the embryonic Everton FC played on between 1879 and 1883.

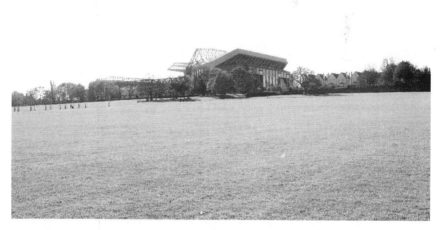

View of Anfield stadium from Stanley Park.

The Kop End at Anfield.

Goodison Park, home ground of Everton FC since 1892. Foregrounded is a statue of William 'Dixie' Dean, legendary Everton goal scorer of the 1920s and 1930s.

Statue outside St Luke's Church and Goodison Park Main Stand dedicated to Everton legends 'The Holy Trinity': Alan Ball, Colin Harvey, and Howard Kendall.

The regalia of the grand officers of English freemasonry. This is the ceremonial attire Houlding would have worn as grand senior deacon of England. *Antiqua Print Gallery/Alamy stock photo.*

John Houlding's first major success in football was to finance the Everton team that won the English League Championship in season 1890–1892. The trophy on the left is the Liverpool Senior Cup, also won by Everton that season. *History and Art Collection/Alamy stock photo.*

Houlding Street, a stone's throw from Anfield stadium and the home of John Houlding's famous Sandon Hotel.

Bust of John Houlding outside Anfield stadium.

Houlding family monument, Everton Cemetery.

4

POLITICAL AMBITIONS CHECKED

John Houlding was now a pivotal figure for the Liverpool Conservative Party. An established councilor of seven years standing for the largest council ward in the city, chairman of the Everton Divisional Council, and the most senior figure in the increasingly influential Working Men's Conservative Association in the north end of Liverpool, he was the effective kingmaker for aspiring Conservative candidates seeking to realise their municipal and parliamentary ambitions. Because of his pivotal position, he had been openly talked of for a number of years as the Tory working-class candidate most likely to go on and represent the city at Westminster, and in so doing, would roll out further the cause of Tory Democracy. In 1885, electoral reform conspired to make that a greater likelihood, and it appeared certain that Houlding's progress through the local ranks would be crowned by his securing of a parliamentary seat. The passing into law of the Redistribution of Seats Act (1885)—a law made to more evenly distribute parliamentary constituencies with the electorate's size—meant that Liverpool increased its number of Westminster seats from three to nine. Both the newly created Everton and Kirkdale seats were up for grabs, and Houlding, as the acknowledged Tory boss in the north end of Liverpool, was an obvious choice for either constituency. Although only a city councillor for just one year, his work in the council chamber was preceded by a decade and a half of dedicated service at all levels of the party, and the momentum was with Houlding.

In Everton, it was perhaps of no surprise that, when Edward Whitley declared himself interested in that seat, Houlding would defer to his mentor, who had pioneered the cause of Conservatism in the district. In neighbouring Kirkdale, however, there were no such complications. The constituency suited Houlding to a tee: an overwhelmingly working-class railyard district that many Evertonians had drifted into for work. This was a district within Houlding's orbit of influence, as his municipal seat encompassed it. He would not find it difficult to convert Kirkdale into a safe Westminster seat for the Conservatives. The Kirkdale Divisional Council, who saw him as an authentic working-class parliamentarian in the making, were also keen to secure Houlding as their candidate. In the event, though, the party leadership opted for another man: a colonial diplomat from outside of the city—Sir George Baden-Powell, brother of Boer War hero and founder of the boy scout movement, Robert Baden-Powell. Obviously, Tory Democracy had some way to go in the 1880s to translate its philosophy of popular Conservatism into the reality of men from humble origins representing the party as MPs. However, Houlding remained ambitious and his chance would come again.

In 1892, another golden opportunity presented itself: the chance to represent his beloved Everton in parliament when Edward Whitley died in early January of that year. However, in the intervening years between 1885 and 1892 the political climate in the city had changed dramatically—and not in a way that favoured John Houlding. Changes in social attitudes to the appropriateness of men involved in the drink trade holding public office left Houlding vulnerable. And the drink issue was made politically explosive by the Liberal Party in 1891, when they weaponised temperance advocacy by adopting the right of local veto as one of its flagship policies (local veto was a pledge that local neighbourhoods would have the right to determine how many licensed premises could operate in their locality rather than a decision made solely at magistrate level). And Houlding's chances of attaining higher office were damaged too by the rise of independent working-class politics. Trade unionist candidates had begun to contest once safe Tory seats, seriously challenging the Conservative claim made in Liverpool that they were the natural home for working class voters. In John Houlding's reaction to these developments we gain an understanding of the frustration he felt as his parliamentary ambitions were blocked. If the John Houlding story up until this point is marked by his success in shaping the environment around him to meet his own needs, in this part of the Houlding story we appreciate the limits to his powers.

HOULDING FIGHTS FOR HIS COUNCIL SEAT—
THE MUNICIPAL CONTEST OF 1891

The first indication that all was not well for Houlding was the autumn council elections of 1891. For the first time since 1884 he had to face the electorate to defend his Everton and Kirkdale council seat, having been given a 'walk-over' in the uncontested 1885 and 1888 council elections. Such was the dominance of the Tories in the ward they were only challenged on two occasions in the decade prior to Houlding's 1891 defence: trouncing their Liberal Party, trade unionist, and Irish Nationalist opponents with thumping majorities. It did not pay for opposition parties to take on Tory Everton's formidable election machine. But things were slowly changing. Inner-Liverpool suburbs like Everton, Kirkdale, West Derby, and Edge Hill housed large artisan populations. Many of the male voters in these areas had some level of skill to their work and would have been members of the growing number of craft trade unions who were at the forefront of a push for independent political representation. The Liberal Party had traditionally articulated the grievances of craft unions, and often stood their politically engaged members as Liberal candidates (so called 'Lib-Lab candidates'). On other occasions the Liberal Party would stand aside and offer party resources to 'stand-alone' trade union candidates. Up and down the country, the 1890s witnessed a rise of trade-union candidates in municipal elections under just such circumstances.

This, then, was the backdrop to John Houlding's delayed appointment with the Everton electorate in 1891. Opposing him was William Nicholson, the secretary of the Liverpool Trade Council, an organisation that would eventually coalesce with other similar regional-based groups to form the Labour Representation Committee—the forerunner to the British Labour Party. The decision to run a labour candidate against Houlding surprised and irritated him. Unlike his fellow Tory councilors in Everton, Houlding was a genuine working-class man made good. He was also president to a number of trade unions. Besides his longstanding presidency of the Liverpool Carters Association, he was also president to the Liverpool Tinplate Workers Union, the Mersey Quay and Railway Carters Union, and the Liverpool Cowkeepers Association. It is clear that Houlding's commitment to trade unions was not merely a means of gaining favour amongst the newly enfranchised working classes. Speaking in Kirkdale in 1890 to an audience of railway workers who were in dispute with their employer, Houlding stated: 'Anyone hearing the hours the railway men are required to work would be satisfied that they had grievances which should be addressed. There are some, however, who take objection to the formation of unions of working men. But ancient history established that right . . . for the purpose of protecting their rights and liberties'.[1]

The implication of the Nicholson challenge, therefore, that he of all people failed to understand and represent the best interests of working men in the district, was taken as a great insult. It undoubtedly irked him throughout the 1891 municipal election campaign, and he was determined to unsettle his challenger by positioning Nicholson as not just a working man's candidate but as a trouble-making radical. Houlding drew a distinction between what *he* saw to be the role of trade unionism and the view of his opponent. He told an election campaign meeting of his supporters: 'Mr Nicholson is the secretary of the Sailors and Firemen's Union. I am the chairman of the Carters Union. I do not, however, try to set the men against their masters, but arbitrate to promote harmony and goodwill between employee and employer'.[2] This was a reference to (and jibe at) the part played by William Nicholson's Liverpool branch of the Sailors Union in bringing about a national strike against ship owners in 1889, a strike won by the union but which was a dispute that rankled other workers in the port whose livelihoods were affected by it. However, Houlding's distinction was gladly seized upon by Nicholson who wished to portray Houlding as someone who—though taking a lead in workers' organisations—'connived' with employers *against* workers. Nicholson accused Houlding in his time as a city councilor of 'sweating' Liverpool Corporation sanitation workers (that is, enforcing harsh terms in pay and conditions upon them). Nicholson claimed that in council committee meetings set to determine the wages of sanitation workers, Houlding was 'always one of the first men to vote in opposition to the interests of labour'.[3] This was a charge angrily dismissed by Houlding. He had, he pointed out in his own defence, increased the wages of sanitary workers of all grades, and promoted men from lower grades to higher grades. Indeed, the approach by Nicholson and his sponsors to target Houlding's record on labour issues does appear to have been fanciful given Houlding's record in negotiating wage settlements satisfactorily on behalf of workers in his capacity as president of four trade union bodies. The Trades Council's decision to target Houlding on this looked a forlorn tactic in this respect. Even if the charges against Houlding had placed him on the defensive, it was a strategy destined for defeat. Help was at hand though from outside the campaign run by the Trades Council and it reinvigorated Nicholson's challenge.

The intervention into the contest of temperance advocate Alexander Guthrie, the most outspoken critic of the drink trade's influence over Liverpool society, placed its outcome in some doubt again. Nicknamed 'Alexander the Less' for his advocacy of temperance in tub-thumping tirades from church and chapel pulpits, Guthrie was the chairman of the Liverpool branch of the United Kingdom Alliance, a national temperance organisation committed to placing legal restraints on brewers and their licensed premises. In a tribute to Guthrie from Liverpool Liberal MP Samuel Smith, the parliamentarian wrote: 'Mr Guthrie has followed a course of life which at times necessarily involved much unpopularity . . . he carried on his work not so much to please his fellow citizens as to satisfy his conscience'.[4] A man, then, about as far removed in character from the charismatic John Houlding as one might imagine. Campaigners like Guthrie had been given a huge stimulus in the aftermath of the publication the year previously of the Reverend Richard Armstrong's 'Deadly Shame of Liverpool'. The Unitarian pastor's pamphlet had rocked Liverpool society and its political classes with its outright condemnation of the Conservative Party leadership, the Liverpool Watch Committee (the police board), and the city's licensing committee; accusing them of being in cahoots with each other and in thrall to the brewing industry—all part of one 'vast, compact interest'[5] which included the city's criminal underworld. It was a sensational attack, and one that the Conservative Party in Liverpool fiercely repudiated; though damage was done to it and the party was on the defensive.

In Houlding's municipal contest Guthrie relished attacking Houlding the brewer. Writing to the *Liverpool Mercury*, Guthrie declared that 'The contest in Everton stands out before all others in interest to temperance and social reformers, for here a direct attack is being made on Great Grog in the person of one his chief captains. Mr Houlding's position is perfectly clear: he stands before the community as the very embodiment of the drink interest'.[6] Houlding had gained this notoriety via his work in a number of drink trade defence associations, particularly for his role as Chairman of the Liverpool Brewers and Wine Spirits Merchants Association where he was the chief campaigner against policing the activities of public houses. One example of this was his lobbying of the city's Watch Committee to resist attempts to curtail the practice of backdoor trading— the practice of selling alcohol beyond the time pubs were licensed to trade. This represented a profitable source of income for pub landlords, but was a practice which temperance reformers found particularly egregious.[7] Guthrie's intervention was a dangerous development for Houlding, as the Tory Party in Liverpool was under huge pressure from reformers to clean up its act with regard to the high levels of criminality and poverty in Liverpool, said to be a result of drunkenness and alcoholism. Indeed, the Liverpool Conservative Party had its own vociferous temperance advocates who could and would seek to make life difficult for Houlding.

Sensing an opportunity, William Nicholson seized the moment to self-identify as a committed temperance man: 'I am a strong supporter of temperance reform' he told a meeting of Liverpool Trades Council and Liberal Party supporters. 'Drink is the greatest drawback to the welfare of the working man'.[8] Some might say this was a fanciful stance, given he was the secretary of the Sailors Union. However, this was a challenge Houlding needed to face down. An opponent calling upon the combined support of the trade council and the temperance lobby, he knew, could run him close, or indeed out of the council chamber all together. His response was to highlight the inconsistency, and what he argued to be the hypocrisy, of his defamers, Guthrie and Nicholson. Addressing a meeting of supporters packed into the Major Street School Hall in Kirkdale, Houlding took aim at his tormentors:

> Mr Guthrie has written to the newspapers asking electors not to support me because I am a brewer. Well, it was not long ago that a bottle was found on the West Coast of Africa and it bore the label 'Bottled by Balfour, Guthrie and Co'. I suppose it is a sin to sell beer in Liverpool but not on the West Coast of Africa. It seems that Mr Guthrie's firm, eight or ten years ago, used to send out shiploads of beer, and the brand was the best known on the West Coast. If Mr Guthrie has not made restitution of the money he made out of that beer, he is speaking under false pretenses.[9]

Houlding's inference of hypocrisy on the part of Guthrie (he, in fact, inherited a bottle making company from his father, who was not a brewer) was a clever ploy that entangled his adversary by indirect association in the 'iniquities' he railed against. Turning his attention to William Nicholson and his seemingly recent conversion to the cause of temperance, Houlding told his supporters of an encounter he said the Trades Council candidate recently had. 'Mr Nicholson has been served with whiskey at a public house, but being informed that Mr Nicholson had not drunk whiskey for twelve years [an earlier claim made by Nicholson], I beg to apologise for the claim I've made. All I can say is that my informant was the lady who served him'—a statement that drew much laughter from those assembled.[10] This was politics with the gloves off, and Houlding's counter attack did the trick, as the drink issue was sidelined for the rest of the campaign.

The election contest had proved to be a bruising and disorienting affair for Houlding: on the defensive over issues that had always before gained him support in the community and at the ballot: his relationship with workers' organisations, and his status as a self-made business man who had overcome obstacles to achieve his goal. These were virtues that had been inverted and turned into vices his opponents taunted him with. In the remaining week of the municipal campaign, however, Houlding went onto the attack, aided by the two largest and most influential groups in Liverpool politics: the Working Men's Conservative Association and the Orange Order. When attacked or placed on the spot, Houlding did what all Liverpool Conservative politicians of the day did—wrapped himself in the flag and declared himself the candidate of the Union of Britain and Ireland, and of the empire, and denounce his opponents as the representative of forces who would do both down. Houlding knew his constituency well enough and he played heavily on the theme that Nicholson—as a 'cats's paw' of 'the radicals'—was a menace to the loyal working men of the district. 'I look upon the Trades Council', he told a Kirkdale Orange Order meeting assembled in his support, 'as nothing but a radical camp in disguise'.[11] On another occasion he informed an Orange meeting: 'I fight the fight of Conservatism and Unionism against all other "isms" that can be brought against us'.[12] As the chairman of a number of Working Men's Conservative Association branches, Houlding expected, and received, the backing of that organisation. It had already warned its own members prior to the 1891 municipal elections to be on guard against 'an extraordinary radical-socialistic-Home Rule combination which will adopt every method of abuse'.[13] Nicholson's tactics against Houlding would have confirmed their predictions. The chairman of the Working Men's Conservative Association, Charles Wycherley, told an audience in Everton that William Nicholson was the willing dupe of the 'Radical Federal Council' who were his 'wire-puller'. 'It is obvious it would cost the labour party far more than it can afford to fight a large ward like Everton. They must be backed by someone, and that fact takes away from Mr Nicholson all title to be a labour candidate'.[14] Nicholson, clearly on the defensive, attempted to respond to the charge by rejecting the notion he was backed by a political organisation and affirmed that he was solely a trade unionist who had come forward in the interests of laboring men. However, the onslaught continued to the 2 November polling day, with claim upon claim being made about Nicholson's political affiliations, the source of his campaign funds, and, indeed, his lack of credibility as a true local man, having resided in Liverpool for only three years.

Nicholson had fought hard, though, and he had the resources of the Trades Council to run an effective campaign, with willing workers on the ground motivated to canvass support amongst fellow trade unionists. In the end Houlding won the election, but only with 7,100 votes to Nicholson's 5,388. It was almost a sensational upset and easily the best showing from a labour or trade-union candidate in the city up to that point. For Houlding, on the other hand, it represented a blow. The contest was closer than most thought it should have been. One explanation offered for the result was that Houlding's poor showing was attributable in no small part to his ongoing difficulties at Everton FC; that his struggle with the membership of that club over its financial affairs and the general direction the club was moving in contributed to the reckoning on polling day, such was the standing of the football club in the district. Certainly, the football club factionalism became a bone of contention during the municipal campaign. Nicholson's supporters used the letters pages of the local press to draw a parallel between what they saw as Houlding's poor conduct in his relations with the membership of Everton FC and the claimed poor contracts he was offering corporation workers.[15] Everton club members continued their own criticism of Houlding via the press too—using Houlding's political discomfort to maximise their case against what they saw as his exploitative club governance:

> Mr Houlding can please himself whether he will exercise his legal rights at the cost of the club or act the part of a generous landlord. [In the event that he didn't take this latter option] the electors of Everton Ward will be asked to consider whether they are satisfied with their

present representative, and if not to take steps to replace him. It will not be a question as between Mr Houlding and the club only, but the thousands of regular visitors to the ground will have to be reckoned with also.[16]

Adding another dimension to the war of words, William Nicholson had a close political relationship with one of Houlding's keenest critics within the Everton FC Committee: Dr William Whitford. As chairman of the Everton and Kirkdale Liberal Association (effectively, John Houlding's political shadow in Everton), Whitford acted as Nicholson's election agent. In the past, Whitford had targeted John Houlding's 'iniquitous' influence as a brewer in the district of Everton.[17]

The *Liverpool Daily Post*, in an editorial published the day after the election, noted the impact of the football cub rift on the outcome of the contest in Everton. 'Mr Houlding's troubles with the football people—a strong body of enthusiasts—was a great blow, and there were few canvassers, even on "King John's" side who did not admit that the dispute cost him a number of votes'.[18] This later led to accusations from Houlding that the final confrontation within Everton FC to determine its leadership and direction was a 'political dodge', and that the breakup of the club was caused ultimately by the meddling of political opponents inside the Everton Committee, aided and abetted by the ubiquitous 'radicals' he had spent his adult life railing against. However, football club factionalism aside, the more damaging hit to Houlding's election campaign came from the questioning of his suitability as a brewer to represent the Everton electorate. Whatever the short-run effects of football club difficulties (and, indeed, whatever challenges he was now faced with from independent working-class politics), it was the attacks from temperance campaigners on the trade that defined his very existence that was most telling as a weapon against him in 1891.

In his victory speech, it was an almost plaintiff John Houlding who told his supporters 'every influence was brought to bear to defeat me because I happen to be a brewer. I do not think it right when it is argued that a man's business means he is not fit to represent you'.[19] He was right to point out that this was a personal attack as well as a political one. Temperance opposition represented a challenge he in particular would have to face for the foreseeable future. Houlding may have seen off the temperance lobby in the municipal contest with an adroit turning of the tables on one of its most vociferous advocates, Alexander Guthrie, but the politician-brewer had made himself a prime target, and his critics did not have long to wait to land another telling blow upon him.

THE EVERTON PARLIAMENTARY CANDIDACY AND THE END OF A DREAM

On 14 January 1892, the sudden death of Edward Whitley, the member of Parliament for Everton, was announced. As John Houlding's erstwhile mentor, he had groomed the younger man to follow in his footsteps in Everton: from councilor to divisional council chairman; and it was widely expected that Houlding would become Whitley's successor for the constituency seat. After a respectful pause of two weeks for the Whitley family's bereavement, the process began to decide the Conservative candidate to fight the byelection in Everton. Learning from his mistake in Kirkdale seven years earlier when, as favourite and local choice for that constituency, he declined to formally declare his interest and was forced by the party leadership to defer, Houlding made it known from the outset that he wished to be Whitley's successor in Everton. Houlding felt, and the Everton divisional council concurred, that his claim was a strong one. His services to the Conservative Party in the district were longstanding and exemplary. His loyalty and commitment to party unity by previously stepping away from a certain safe seat in parliament was well remembered. The time and effort he gave to the governance of local social institutions, which were crucial to the population of the north end of Liverpool, was acknowledged and to his credit. Though his recent performance in the local council elections was shaky, the Liberal Party were weak in the parliamentary district and their electoral organisation was no match for the Tory machine. It is true that a threat remained ever-present from temperance agitators, but only a failure of nerve on the part of the Liverpool Conservative leadership could prevent a Houlding candidacy running smoothly through to victory. Unfortunately for Houlding that was exactly what happened.

Right from the beginning of the process, Houlding had a fight on his hands to be declared the party's constituency candidate. Another Conservative, James Lowry, put himself forward in the days after Houlding threw his hat into the ring. A food wholesaler from Toxteth, a district on the other side of the city, Lowry had none of the local support of John

Houlding. Indeed, as a Methodist and a man from Liverpool's south end he had little in common with the predominantly working-class Anglicans of Everton. His danger to Houlding, however, was that he was also a temperance advocate. Lowry's intervention changed the dynamic of the selection process by fueling concerns that Conservative unity in Everton would be threatened to a point where a Liberal candidate could contest the byelection and take the seat. Lowry's move placed a huge question mark over the wisdom of selecting Houlding. In a general election year (which 1892 was), the Tories would be facing a reinvigorated national Liberal Party under the leadership of Liverpool-born William Ewart Gladstone. The Liberal grassroots organisation required to take the fight to the Tories on the doorstep was much bolstered by the support of the United Kingdom Alliance, the national temperance movement with their zealous army of campaigners. The Liberals were committed to bringing forward prohibition legislation which, if elected to power, would curtail drastically the issuing of liquor licenses. Already in Liverpool the effect of the Liberal ground campaign on Tory fortunes had become apparent, with the Liberals seeing a surge in support for their candidates in the recently held autumn municipal elections, when, as we have seen, John Houlding experienced a huge scare.

Internally, Liverpool's Conservative Party was torn over their historically close connections to the drink industry. The leadership were beholden to brewers for financial support, but their instincts were to act strategically in order to retain power and return Conservative MPs to parliament—its number-one priority. And the pressure for them to intervene over Houlding's Everton nomination increased when the Everton Divisional Council was petitioned by a Conservative Party temperance group. That body had written a letter to the Divisional Council (subsequently published in the local press) stating: 'At a meeting of temperance Conservatives it was resolved to express to you the great regret which is felt that your executive should contemplate adopting a candidate who is directly associated with the drink traffic'. Houlding's candidacy, they went on, would be 'little short of a disaster . . . in a year which can only be described both locally and nationally as one of crisis. In case your executive should adopt such a candidate, a considerable and influential section feel it necessary to bring forward an independent temperance Conservative candidate, a course which it is trusted will be obviated by a wise selection on the part of your committee'.[20]

This downbeat assessment (and threat) to advancing Houlding for Everton was underlined by letters to the city's Conservative-leaning newspaper, the *Liverpool Courier*. One incredulous correspondent asked, 'Do the Conservative leaders in Everton seriously contemplate the temperance crusade that would be commenced and carried on against Mr Houlding and the Conservative Party and that nothing would please our radical, Home Rule friends more than that Mr Houlding be the selected Conservative candidate'.[21] Another letter writer urged caution in choosing Houlding based on claimed changes in the demographic profile of the constituency—changes which made Houlding apparently less representative of the district than he once was. 'There are two important facts which must not be lost sight of. First, the political complexion of Everton has changed very considerably within the past ten-to-fifteen years. Streets that were filled with Protestants and Conservatives of the working class in those days are now partially occupied, or are occupied, by Roman Catholics and Radicals. Second, I know something of the drift of temperance opinion in Everton, and how for many years I have watched the steady advance and growth of that opinion, and I have no hesitation in saying that to press his [Houlding's] claims at the present moment will only lead to disaster'.[22] As the correspondent indicated, there had indeed been an influx of many better-off Catholics from the dockside districts of north Liverpool settling in Everton. In fact, by 1892 Everton had one of the largest Roman Catholic populations in Liverpool outside of the traditional Catholic stronghold area of the dockland communities. With just one church in Everton in 1851, the Roman Catholic Church, responding to the greater migration of Catholics from the Parish of Liverpool into the district, had established four parish churches there by 1892: St Edwards, St Francis Xavier, Our Lady Immaculate, and St Joseph's. Much of the Roman Catholic population in the district was initially concentrated in west Everton neighbourhoods: Netherfield and Everton Village, bordering the parish of Liverpool. In some ecclesiastical districts Catholics constituted over one-third of those surveyed for religious worship, though elsewhere in Everton their presence was marginal, ranging between 10 per cent and 15 per cent of the population.[23]

Regardless of the advance of nontraditional Conservative supporters into the district, it was the mood within Tory ranks that would determine Houlding's fate, and this began to turn significantly against him when a *Liverpool Courier* editorial undermined his credibility as a unity candidate: 'Few men have worked longer or more resolutely on behalf of Conservatism than Mr John Houlding', it encouragingly began.

> But local Conservatives have too high opinion of Mr Houlding's party fealty and attachment to Conservative principles to believe that he will allow any personal claims to interfere with the united action and the consequent success of Conservatism in Everton. The party of disruption [the Liberal Party] are watchful and will seize any advantage to strengthen the plans of Mr Gladstone, which, if not checked, will end in the dismemberment of the empire.[24]

The thinly coded message was almost a personal letter to Houlding himself: pushing the buttons they knew would nag at his conscience concerning Tory unity, opposition to radicalism, and defence of empire. The pushback against Houlding forced the Everton Divisional Council to add two more names to the list of candidate hopefuls in an effort to take the heat off themselves. Local ship owner and former MP for Birkenhead, David MacIver, and Lord Claud Hamilton, the one-time MP for Liverpool West Derby, were approached to join Houlding to contest the seat. However, the Divisional Council appear to have deliberately approached men who could not or would not compete with Houlding. Lord Claud Hamilton made it plain that he was uninterested in the Everton Divisional Council's approach, while David MacIver stated that 'I would not decline to contest the seat against any outsider, but I am one of those that recognises the claims of Mr John Houlding and believe that the constituency ought, if possible, be represented by a local man'.[25] The Everton Divisional Council were on a collision course with the city party leadership, and a full-blown Conservative crisis in their premier parliamentary constituency was on the cards.

It was at this moment that John Houlding made the most important decision of his political career: he withdrew his name from the candidate's list. He knew that if he persevered with his claims for the Everton seat he would have made it almost impossible for the Liverpool party leadership to deny him it. His path to parliament would have been difficult for any Liberal candidate to block (fighting a seat in what was known as 'the Conservative Gibraltar of Liverpool' was an onerous task). In all likelihood, the attitude of the party leadership must have been a huge influence on Houlding's decision not to run. As he had proven by withdrawing from the contest for the vacant Kirkdale seat in 1885, Houlding was nothing if not a loyal party man, and any groundswell of opinion that his contesting Everton would aid the opposition—the hated radicals—undoubtedly would have influenced his decision to drop out. Informing the Everton Divisional Council of his decision, Houlding found a convenient excuse to withdraw from the race in an effort to avoid further conflict within the party. 'I have thought the matter over very seriously, and although it would be crowning the edifice after the laborious twenty-five years I have worked for Everton, still I must also consider that I am not so young as I was. When I see old friends dying around me it makes me consider whose turn will be next. My medical adviser tells me that with care I may live a number of years to be of use, and knowing as I do the long and wearying hours an MP has to work in the House of Commons if he does his duty, I think it would not be advisable for me to undertake that duty. And whilst again thanking you for the high honour you have conferred on me by selecting me as one of three to submit for your selection, I must object to my name going any further'.[26]

Houlding's decision was reluctantly accepted by the Everton Divisional Council, and the search for a candidate eventually settled upon the name of James Willox, the proprietor of the Tory-supporting *Liverpool Courier*. But Houlding's explanation for withdrawal was less than convincing. The widely held view was that he had been coerced into dropping his claims on the seat by the party leadership. An editorial in the *Liverpool Mercury* caught the mood of suspicion. 'Mr Arthur Forwood, MP [Liverpool's Tory leader] is said to be wholly engaged in the task of upsetting every selection or decision made by the local members of his party. In Everton, as is pretty well understood, the candidature of Mr John Houlding would have met with unanimous support from the organised branches of the Constitutional Association; but as Mr Houlding was not acceptable to the heads of the party he had to step down. A large section of the Conservative Party in the Everton division has become estranged. Mr James Willox, whose journalistic services to the Tory Party in this city are well known, is selected and now seen as the best way out of a serious difficulty. He is likely to reconcile the differences which have recently arisen in their ranks owing to the discountenance given at headquarters to the proposed candidature of Mr Houlding, whose numerous friends are still chafing over the rebuff he was met with'.[27] Two days later the same newspaper rammed the point home again for good measure:

Mr Forwood's efforts were made to prevent Mr John Houlding from being adopted as the late Mr Whitley's successor. Mr Houlding was, as is well known, quite prepared to accept parliamentary honours, to which, indeed, he felt he had some claim after the zealous services he has rendered his party during the last quarter of a century; and he had a host of friends in Everton who would have worked and voted for him and will doubtless share in his disappointment that his candidature was opposed by the Constitutional Association.[28]

Notwithstanding that the *Liverpool Mercury* (a Liberal-leaning newspaper) was likely making political mischief over Tory factionalism, their analysis appears to be sustainable. Even the newly chosen Tory candidate for Everton, James Willox, was seemingly unable to maintain the pretence that Houlding's age and state of health had led to his withdrawal from the Everton race. In his maiden speech to the Everton Divisional Council days after being chosen as their candidate, Willox conceded: 'I have a special debt of obligation to express to Mr Houlding for an act of self-abnegation which is rarely found in public men these days'.[29] Quite obviously the consensus was that Houlding had been persuaded to deny his own ambitions.

Houlding dutifully supported Willox's candidature. In the event, there was no byelection, as the Liberals declined to face Willox who then immediately became Everton's MP. Later in July of that year Houlding ran Willox's General Election campaign—a fight Willox duly won by soundly defeating his Liberal opponent, Peter Atkin. Indeed, Houlding's relationship with Willox appears to have been a warm one. There was no hint of personal rancor in Houlding's acceptance of Willox as a man who, in effect, was handed what he thought would be his parliamentary seat, even though it must surely have occurred to him that Willox's *Liverpool Courier* had lobbied hard for Houlding to stand down from his claims for the constituency, and that there may have been a calculation on Willox's part to secure the seat for himself. A rapport developed quickly between the two men, exemplified in Willox and Houlding cofounding a masonic lodge (Sir Walter Raleigh Lodge). However, this is not to say that Houlding was less than furious over his treatment by the city party leadership, and his frustrations boiled over on the occasion of Willox's formal confirmation as Everton candidate, carried out at a special congress of the ruling Constitutional Association.

Chaired by the formidable Sir Arthur Forwood (described by the Liverpool Liberal Party leader, Sir Robert Holt, as being 'short of the instincts of a Gentleman'[30]), it was a meeting that proved to be a seminal moment for the Liverpool Conservative Party and the forces shaping its future. Before the newly selected candidate for Everton, James Willox, was officially accepted, Houlding rose to address the assembly and suggested that, given the trampling over of the Everton Divisional Council's choice of its preferred original candidate, it was incumbent upon the chair of the Constitutional Association to provide a clarification on the correct procedure of choosing parliamentary candidates. This request by Houlding, though, brought forth a prolonged and stinging rebuke from Arthur Forwood, which took what should have been a simple coronation of James Willox onto an issue of much greater importance: party democracy. In an exchange that almost certainly destroyed any future aspirations Houlding might still have harboured for a place in parliament, Forwood stated that it was a divisional council's right *only* to present a shortlist of candidates for the perusal of the party leadership, *not* their place to adopt a candidate to run for parliament. However, Houlding did not back off. He knew there were powerful men in the room from the Working Men's Conservative Association who backed his questioning of the city's Tory leader. Referring back to the Constitutional Association's existing rules, Houlding extrapolated: 'I do not think it says this committee has the power to say "yea" or "nay"; it simply says "we" [the divisional councils] are to "consult" with the executive committee of the Constitutional Association. It does not give you the autocratic power to say "yea" or "nay"'.[31] Houlding's dramatic intervention clearly underlined the enormous sense of anger and disappointment which had been building within him after two opportunities to become an MP had been denied him by the grandees of the city party. To declare that Forwood was acting as an 'autocrat' was, he knew, the effective end to any notions of him becoming an MP in Liverpool. The real significance of the confrontation, though, was to crystalise latent tensions that existed between the Tory Party leadership who controlled the Constitutional Association (the party's governing body), and the Working Men's Conservative Association (who held sway over rank-and-file Tory members) over what each side felt constituted 'Tory Democracy'—the credo upon which the party enjoyed unbroken success in Liverpool for decades.

HOULDING—A MAN OUT OF HIS TIME

A new schism was about to develop in Liverpool Conservatism concerning the rights of district associations to assert their free will, unfettered from an overbearing 'Dale Street clique', as the party leadership were unflatteringly described (Dale Street in Liverpool was the street on which the offices of the Constitutional Association were located). The division, ostensibly, was also a doctrinal one. The Working Men's Conservative Association and Orange Order were set on pushing their sectarian agenda. They argued that the integrity of the Union depended on checking the advance of 'Romanising' influences (that is, Catholic influences), and that religious affairs were the central issue of the day for the Conservative Party, not only in Liverpool but nationally. The party leadership were viewed to be more sanguine on the issue, placing party before Protestantism. Arthur Forwood was mocked by the Liverpool Orange Order as 'the political Pope of Dale Street',[32] but, in reality, there was no fundamental difference of opinion on religious matters, and the Liverpool Tory leadership were supporters of the various Church Discipline Bills sponsored by the Liverpool Working Men's Conservative Association that passed through parliament with the aim of prosecuting 'ecclesiastical offences' by Church of England clergy. The real problem for Forwood was that the issue was bound up with a grab for power being made by party grassroots organisations, such as the Working Men's Conservative Association, and the decentralisation of power in the Liverpool party. Any move in that direction would be resisted.

Houlding was not a willing or natural participant in such divisive matters. For the most part, nondoctrinal and erring towards compromise within the party, he respected hierarchies too much to want to bring about change that would threaten the governing order in Liverpool and beyond. His questioning of the Liverpool party leadership was merely to clarify party procedure so that everyone knew where they stood within the hierarchy and what was possible and what was not. He was, nevertheless, and despite his best wishes, drawn into the fray. The denial of Houlding's claims on Everton became fuel for those at odds with Forwood and the Constitutional Association. After the crushing of his parliamentary ambitions, the last thing Houlding needed was more conflict in his political life. Ironically, at the centre of his new troubles would be his lifelong friend, Thomas McCracken. McCracken was deputy grand master of the

Liverpool Orange Order and a member of Everton Conservative Division Council. A longtime critic of the party leadership, McCracken was so incensed at how the local party in Everton had been treated over the Houlding candidature he independently declared himself a Conservative candidate for Sir Edward Whitley's vacant Everton municipal seat. McCracken told a meeting of his supporters: 'For too long you have been hoodwinked to keep certain men in positions of self-aggrandisement. Political life in Dale Street is ruled by one man whose name I will not mention [Sir Arthur Forwood]. . . . We put up John Houlding. Well, John Houlding is a dear friend of mine, and he told me his great ambition was to be a member of parliament. But a voice from Dale Street shouted "Clear Out!". I am not going to tolerate the crushing of my independence any longer'.[33] As a demonstration of loyalty towards him, it was completely unwelcomed by John Houlding. Though himself being at odds with the party leadership he could not, as a man who had cause of late to question the arbitrary application of party rules, accept McCracken's unilateral declaration that he would run for Whitley's council seat. The slate of candidates was to be determined and Houlding, as chairman of the Everton Conservative Association, rejected his old friend's self-nomination. In reality, it was poor calculation to think that John Houlding would be anything other than loyal to the Conservative Party. Regardless of frustrations over his own thwarted ambitions, his adult life had been devoted to the party of church, state, and empire. No independent declaration would be tolerated by him.

With the door slammed shut on him, McCracken was forced to run as an independent in the council byelection, but was duly defeated by the official Conservative Party candidate, ship-owner Ralph Leyland. The choice of Leyland (an outsider to the district) was seen as further confirmation that the party's leadership were determined to rule by decree and deny local democratic decision making. However, change was in the air and the balance of forces in the party was shifting quickly and decisively away from its centre towards the Working Men's Conservative Association. Months after McCracken's defeat in Everton by Leyland, the latter was dropped by the party leadership for the autumn municipal elections in favour of Austin Taylor, the founder of the staunchly Protestant Layman's League and a man in the vanguard of sectarian politics in the city. It was more evidence of Conservative politics in Liverpool pivoting away from being the party of gradual social reform towards a more aggressive playing of the sectarian card. As much as the party leadership under Arthur Forwood sought to keep control over their Orange Order and Working Men's Conservative Association, it was on the wrong side of history. The Tory Party in Liverpool was in the process of fusing its traditional Unionist credentials to a brand of Protestant militancy—a change underlined by Forwood's increasing reliance on the Working Men's Conservative Association to maintain Tory control of the city council. Forwood would soon be replaced as effective leader of the Liverpool Tories by the Working Men's Conservative Association's chairman, Sir Archibald Tutton Salvidge. Salvidge, the managing director of Bents Brewery, eventually took the presidency of the Constitutional Association and dominated the Liverpool party until his death in 1928. In this new and ideologically charged era, a more pragmatic old school Tory like John Houlding found it increasingly difficult to remain relevant.

The six-month period from October 1891 to March 1892, taking in the two Everton municipal elections and the saga of Edward Whitley's successor as MP for Everton, marked the beginning of the end of John Houlding's political ascendancy within the Liverpool Conservative Party. The undisputed 'governor' of Everton had been diminished as a man who had all too easily been overlooked for a parliamentary seat. And for some rank-and-file Tories in the district he was also viewed as a man who the party grandees could look to in order to bring to heel activists discontented with the trampling of party democracy. This decline in his political status, though, should not be exaggerated; Houlding was still held in regard by most sections of the party and he retained his civic popularity. In fact, Thomas McCracken, the longstanding friend Houlding had need to turn against in the council byelection of 1892, continued to remain close to him, joining him on trips abroad and becoming part of Houlding's entourage at Houlding's soon-to-be new venture, Liverpool FC.[34] However, his political route forward had been blocked, and the future was now in the hands of men willing to go with the flow of the ideological forces now dictating the Liverpool Conservative Party's agenda. King John had been sidelined in his own kingdom.

* * *

All told, 1892 was a year to forget for Houlding. It ended with the loss of one of his closest friends and political allies, Dr Dunlop Costine. On top of his own travails, it was a huge body blow for Houlding. He and Dr Costine had, over the previous quarter of a century, made their way through the various ranks of the Conservative Party in the north end of the city; Houlding had gone on to become a councilor and chairman of the Everton Conservative Association, Dr Costine had become chairman of the Kirkdale Conservative Association. The two men were also guardians at the West Derby Union and socialised together: Houlding made a point of joining Dr Costine each Sunday evening on a night out to the theatre or else to a tavern. A close bond existed between the men. The *Liverpool Mercury* described Houlding's demeanour when speaking at an Everton Conservative Association meeting called to express its sympathy on Dr Costine's passing as 'showing in voice and manner how deeply he was affected'. Addressing his audience, Houlding confessed:

> This is one of the saddest things that could have happened. I found him to be one of those few men fit to stand before a monarch or a peasant. He prevented offence by his gentleness and his courtesy of expression, notwithstanding that he always spoke his mind in a straight forward manner. . . . He was about the last of my old friends that I have gathered along my way in this world, and they are very hard to replace when a man gets to my time of life.[35]

This is quite a revealing portrayal: highlighting a softer, less harsh side to Houlding's persona. Perhaps his tone and his words about his friend can be seen as a hankering for an earlier, less divisive time in politics than the increasingly rancorous internal party wrangling he was now faced with. It is certainly a wistful look backward. We might also speculate that Houlding's own nagging spells of ill health—first reported in the local press in early 1890 and described as 'bronchial' in nature[36]—were beginning to impose upon his mood. All in all, the sense of control and assured progress that had marked Houlding's rise to prominence over the previous three decades seemed to be undermined as his sixtieth year approached.

The football club agitation against him was part and parcel of the funk that Houlding found himself mired in too. The Everton FC factional struggle had reared its head in Houlding's campaign to retain his municipal seat at the end of 1891. At the precise moment of his political crisis—sensing his vulnerability—his opponents in the club chose to launch a public assault on their president, something not lost on John Houlding. The future of the 'Good Old Club' was vexatious for him. However, here at least he could continue to exert a great degree of control via his investment. His association with the club ensured that he maintained a high public profile in the City of Liverpool too. As one observer bemoaned: 'In Liverpool, it is football and footballers who are more discussed . . . council and imperial parliament matters sink into insignificance in most company when the great winter game is on tap'.[37] It was here, not in the world of politics, that Houlding would go on to establish his longest lasting legacy. First, though, he had to cut through the Gordian Knot of an acrimonious standoff with the Everton FC Committee.

5

THE FOUNDATION OF LIVERPOOL FOOTBALL CLUB

On 25 January 1892—without the knowledge of the Everton Committee—John Houlding moved to secure his investment in Everton FC by registering the organisation as a business: The Everton Football Club and Athletic Grounds Company. The timing of this dramatic development coincided with what Houlding and his allies at the club saw as underhand methods by his enemies on the club committee to unseat him from Everton FC. The political attack on an exposed Houlding during the municipal elections of autumn 1891 and his candidacy for the Everton parliamentary seat in January 1982 were interpreted as the actions of men who would not countenance coexistence with him. At that point, Houlding daringly seized the initiative. Predictably, the move was met with vigorous protest from the Everton Committee, which denounced his grab for the club as the actions of a despot. This condemnation was followed up days later with the declaration that they too, the club committee, were to register Everton FC as a business, and they confidently predicted that the club members and the game's authorities would recognise only their claims to represent Everton FC. The Rubicon had been crossed by Houlding, there would be no turning back from this point.

THE SPLIT OF EVERTON FC

Houlding's audacious gambit, he knew, stood little chance of success, given that the vast majority of the membership sided with the committee, and that the Football League would see fit to back *only* the officially elected club committee. However, he also knew the time left to the end of the season in March—which the committee had stated would be the club's last season at Anfield—presented him with an opportunity to concentrate minds on a solution to the club's governance crisis on his terms. Failing the success of that plan, the period also allowed him the chance to persuade away as many of the large Everton membership to back him in a new football club venture at the current stadium, Anfield, and forsake those seeking to leave for pastures new.

The first strategy—a solution to the club crisis by continuing negotiations with the club committee—was, by this stage, a very difficult one to pull off, given the toxicity of relations between the president and his entourage and the majority on the club committee. As was mentioned earlier, Houlding's limited liability scheme to purchase John Orrell's adjoining land in order to preserve the stadium had been summarily rejected by the membership. However, the Everton Committee, seeking to move the club to a new location, were faced with a tough task of their own in trying to convince hundreds of reluctant members to ditch the club's fixed assets. Interwoven with this were fears that the club's 'brand identity' would be harmed by shifting away from an Anfield home the team had become synonymous with. As one club member, a Mr Everett, put it in a letter to the *Liverpool Daily Post*: 'What businessmen would move his business to new premises from premises where he has commanded wonderful success, to effect a saving in rental? The gain is not worth the risk'.[1] Anfield was integral to the identity of Everton FC, one of the best-known sporting venues in the country and which also played host to England international matches.

Recognising this hesitancy, and the possibility of remaining at Anfield with a compromise deal, Houlding tested the resolve of the committee by offering more negotiations, this time concerning the raised level of rent. The major trigger for discontent had been the insistence by Houlding for the club to meet the rental increase of £250 per annum—which represented the 4 per cent interest payment Houlding asked the now successful Everton FC to pay on his initial £6,000 outlay he made in 1885 to secure the land the stadium stood upon. Houlding's revised offer was to row back on his own rental demands to below the full rate of interest, an offer that took into consideration his renegotiation with John Orrell in which he concluded a deal for the club to pay £120 per annum rental for Orrell's adjacent land in order to avoid his neighbour disturbing the club's grandstand. Though not meeting the committee's demands that their president, as the man who had made the initial transaction with Joseph Orrell, bear the unforeseen extra costs, it did amount to a substantial improvement on long-term security of tenure and rental costs. From Houlding, there was a willingness to revert to his pre-1888 position of accepting a lower rental rate *and* a new written commitment not to disturb the tenancy of the club; from Orrell there was a commitment to provide the club with a ten-year lease for an annual rental fee of £120. The deal, if accepted, would hand Everton FC secure and stable tenure for the foreseeable future.

A special general meeting called to discuss the Houlding offer decided on the following response: 'That the Everton Football Club offer to Mr Houlding £180 per annum rental and that £120 per annum be offered to Mr Orrell on a lease to run for ten years, the terms to be as mentioned by Mr Houlding, except that he shall not have a nominee on the committee'.[2] This counteroffer—resulting in a fixed-loss on rental *and* the elimination of his influence within the governing body of the club—would, its architects knew, be unacceptable to Houlding. His rejection of the committee's counterproposal marked the effective end of negotiations between him and the club committee. The process, though, would have shown to wavering club members with residual sympathy for the club president that he was seeking compromise, which is what his newly constituted financial offer was no doubt designed to convey.

However, the greater part of Houlding's strategy in the early months of 1892 was to draw the club membership's attention towards what he argued to be the politically motivated opposition he was facing from within the club committee; to present the agitation he met there not primarily as a financial disagreement but a 'political dodge'. This was a charge Houlding first made in the autumn of 1891 during his municipal election campaign, when the club's governance problems were used by opponents in an attempt to embarrass him. It was a charge the club committee firmly repudiated. However, there was certainly enough circumstantial evidence for Houlding to point to in order to back up his claim. There was, after all, a phalanx of Liberal Party activists on the Everton

Committee. George Mahon, Dr William Whitford, Dr James Clement
Baxter, William Clayton, and Alfred Riley Wade were all involved in
Liberal Party district associations.[3] In the words of an inflammatory editorial in the Liberal-leaning *Liverpool Daily Post*, these were men who
had 'taken it upon themselves to rid the club of an influence that had
apparently grown stronger year after year'.[4]

The 'influence' the *Daily Post* referred to extended beyond Houlding
to a number of other men taking up honourary and administrative positions within Everton FC—men who also held positons in the city's drink-
trade defence associations. Two men in particular exercised the concerns
of the Everton Committee: club auditor, Simon Jude, and club solicitor,
Edwin Berry. Simon Jude was the secretary of the Liverpool Brewers and
Wine Spirits Merchants Association, a body Houlding was chairman of;
Edwin Berry, a longstanding member of Everton FC who had acted for
many years as its solicitor and vice president, was solicitor to the Liverpool Licensed Victuallers Association and was employed by many of the
largest breweries in the city of Liverpool to fight their cases through the
magistrates courts. If these leading lights of the drink trade had their
hands on the levers of control at the club—a club on the cusp of incorpo-
ration—the likelihood was that its ownership would fall into the clutches
of the drink trade, as football clubs up and down the country had already
done.

To men like Whitford and Mahon the presence of Houlding, Berry,
and Jude in the hierarchy of such a well-respected institution as Everton
FC was intolerable. Both men had longstanding political grudges against
Houlding. Whitford, the Everton Liberal Association chairman, clashed
often and publically with Houlding concerning the latter's drink trade
connections. A surgeon and justice of the peace, Whitford gave frequent
lectures in Liverpool on the proliferation of the drink interest and its
danger to the community. The *Liverpool Review* dubbed Whitford 'the
elect hero of the fire and sword teetotalers' for his consistent attacks on
the Liverpool Police force and the licensing bench who had failed, as he
saw it, to crack down on publicans operating outside of the law. Another
city weekly journal less flatteringly called him 'a crank on the eternal
liquor question'.[5]

George Mahon was, perhaps, John Houlding's most dogged opponent
at the club. Mahon was a senior partner in Roose, Mahon, & Howorth, a
leading Liverpool accountancy firm and was, by all accounts, a learned

man who 'occasionally lectured on microscopic and astronomical studies'.[6] Mahon had credibility, and the air of a man who simply and dispassionately dealt in facts. He was the most able of all Houlding's critics to ramp up the narrative that the club president was intent on the exploitation of Everton for his own personal gain. In particular, he articulated fears that Houlding and his associates sought to incorporate the club and open it up to the control of brewers. Mahon made it plain throughout the dispute that he and his colleagues were determined to ensure that the drink trade's advances into the club would be checked under a new regime set up away from the president and his aides. Speaking at a subcommittee meeting prior to the club's historic split from Houlding, Mahon assured 'the friends of the club and outsiders' that they vowed 'not to sell intoxicating liquors on the [new] ground'.[7]

Mahon, a member of Walton Liberal Association, had an ongoing feud with Houlding. In 1889, in his capacity as returning officer for the Walton Division of Lancashire County Council, he had incensed Houlding, the election agent for Tory candidate Sir David Radcliffe, by rejecting Radcliffe's nomination to contest the Walton seat on a technicality (Radcliffe's application had apparently been lodged too late to be passed). Houlding openly accused Mahon of political sabotage, further complaining that bill posters bearing Mahon's name 'had been used to cover a large number of posters announcing Conservative Party meetings' in support of Radcliffe in Walton. Commenting on the incident, the Liberal-leaning *Bootle Times* stated that Mahon's decision to disqualify Sir David Radcliffe 'would be lamented by publicans and others inasmuch as it deprives them of a man who would most likely maintain their interests'.[8] A war of words erupted between the two men and this incident set the tone for their future relationship within Everton FC.

It was not, then, difficult for Houlding and his friends to sustain their charge that a political plot had been hatched to unseat him at Everton FC. And in the early months of 1892, Houlding's preemptive strike in positioning the Everton Committee as political wreckers of a sporting institution was gaining some traction. The local newspapers printed letters from correspondents identifying themselves as club members who were clearly suspicious of the motives of those at the vanguard of the attack on Houlding and his allies. One letter to the *Liverpool Courier* from a member who attended a meeting called ostensibly to discuss arrangements for a charity athletic event to be held at Anfield claimed that it had been hijacked by men seeking to politicise the ongoing club dispute: 'I have acted with these men in the past', the correspondent declared, 'believing them to be sincere and having the welfare of Everton Football Club at heart. It is now plain that political rancor is at the bottom of the movement, and I shall offer every resistance to any further development of those plans'. Another letter to the *Courier* made the 'political dodge' claim in a slightly more nuanced way: 'I trust you will grant me a little space to warn members [of Everton FC] against the seductive influences of debating society oratory to which they have been treated at the general meetings of the club, and to remind them that in the movement of a club an approved businessman is of much more value than who those possessing the eloquence of John Bright' (Bright was a nineteenth-century radical Liberal politician who campaigned against the Corn Laws).[9]

The playing out of the political dimension to the club's troubles in the public domain in this manner was only to Houlding's benefit. But did it have any tangible effect? If we consider that the newly incorporated Everton FC months after the split of the club drew to its side 340 of the club's 500-plus members, then the answer could well be yes, or at least that the Everton Committeemen had perhaps overstated their claims to represent the 'vast majority' of the membership of the club. However, whatever the impact had been, it was not enough to prevent the rupture of the club, and in a last dramatic showdown with his enemies at an emergency meeting of the club membership, Houlding submitted to the inevitable.

The meeting was called on 15 March 1892 at the Presbyterian school meeting rooms on Royal Street, Everton to hear a no-confidence motion in Houlding and to consider resolutions for both his removal from office and the removal of those men left on the committee who had supported his registering Everton FC as a limited company without the knowledge and consent of the committee. The outcome was, in truth, a formality. A decision was made to expel the president; his right-hand man, John James Ramsey; and two other loyal committeemen, Alexander Nisbet and Thomas Howarth. Even at such a moment, though, Houlding's status was recognised when one of his chief accusers, George Mahon, offered him the chairmanship of the meeting. In response, Houlding defiantly responded 'I am here to reply, and a criminal never takes the chair, he stops in the dock'.[10] Loud applause and laughter rang around the hall. It was obvious from Houlding's reply that he was underlining the severity of his treatment at the hands of the committee. The reception his words received suggests that, even amongst the members of the club who were supporting their committee's resolve to expel Houlding, there was recognition of the crucial part he had played in Everton FC's rise to preeminence. The departing John Houlding deserved at least that much.

* * *

In truth, and despite his long association with Everton FC, Houlding had been something of a gatecrasher; a man at odds with the sensibility of the club. For all of his charismatic leadership and financial clout there was always a feeling that his presence at Everton conflicted with the moral authority of the club, held in the hands of others such as Alfred Riley Wade and William Cuff. These men were founding members of Everton back in the late 1870s; indeed, they were ex-players of the team and would go on to become key players in the club's future at Goodison Park. Later arrivals to the club and, indeed, to the club committee, like George Mahon and William Whitford, were much more compatible with these men and the founding principles of the club they embodied. It was this clash of cultures at the club that created tension throughout Houlding's time as president, and it eventually led to his removal.

However, he had a vision of another football project, and he had the men he could call upon to make his vision a reality. He also, of course, had Anfield. On 18 March 1892, just three days after the Everton split, Houlding sought permission from the game's authorities to register the name 'The Liverpool Association Football Club'.[11] The name 'Liverpool Football Club' had been tried by football clubs in the city before, without the necessary wherewithal and swagger to back up such a bold project. John Houlding had both commodities in spades. He would set up a very different form of organisation to the one he had been shown the door of. A new era was about to dawn, and John Houlding had a score to settle with Everton FC.

THE LIVERPOOL FOOTBALL AND ATHLETICS GROUND COMPANY

Houlding wasted no time in responding to his expulsion from Everton. Barely two weeks later he was at the city's Neptune Hotel in Clayton Square surrounded by the newly assembled executive committee of the

Liverpool Football Club. It was reported that the financial prospects of
the fledgling club were good and that several first-rate players were in
negotiations with a view to playing in the upcoming 1892–1893 season.[12]
By registering the club immediately after the old season had ended and
buying professional players, mostly from Scotland, Houlding hoped to
prove to the Football League that his new club were at least worthy of
taking a spot in the league's Second Division tier, which had recently
been created. Twelve clubs would be invited to play in the Second Division's inaugural season. It was typical of Houlding that he felt he could
catapult an organisation with no competitive playing pedigree ahead of
many of the game's established football clubs, such as Bootle, Sheffield
United, Small Heath (Birmingham City), and Ardwick (Manchester
City). In the event, Houlding's early ambition for Liverpool FC was
thwarted and the club entered the Lancashire League for its first season in
existence where they would play teams like Southport, Higher Walton,
Fleetwood Rangers, and Heywood Central—minnows of the Lancashire
football scene who would be no real match for the team of professional
players that Houlding had, by the close season's end, assembled for the
Liverpool team. Patience would be required.

In the meantime, Houlding got on with the task of constructing the
contours of his new club. It would be very different to Everton. The most
important difference of all would be that John Houlding would have total
control over Liverpool FC. Unsurprisingly, given his experience at Everton, he left nothing to chance in this new venture with regard to club
governance. The commercial rights of the board and the concentration of
power in their hands were immediately enshrined at Liverpool FC. One
rule established was that 'The office of director shall not be vacated by
his being concerned or participating in the profits of supplying the company with any goods or stock'. Another rule stated that 'The Executive
Committee should have sole control over the ground and finances, power
to engage players, arrange fixtures and of all matters including the election of members during its year in office'.[13] On the matter of ownership,
from the outset Houlding figured prominently as a shareholder. In 1892,
there were only forty-seven original subscribers to Liverpool FC, and
John Houlding controlled just under half of the initial 788 shares in the
club; easily the biggest single source of take up. By the end of his time at
Liverpool a decade later, he controlled over two-thirds of the club shares
(1,960 of 2,953).[14] The Houlding shares were owned by John himself and

his daughter Alice-Margaret and son William, but this was unquestionably John Houlding's show.

By contrast, the newly formed Everton Football Club Company limited had its 2,263 shares distributed a lot more evenly across a large membership. With 453 original subscribers, the average shareholdings in the club remained low; each shareholder averaging between four to five shares, and the original ten directors of Everton owned just 6 per cent of club shares.[15] With a system of one share–one vote, this amounted to an attempt to carry over into the limited company era the structure of a members' club and, theoretically at least, democratic control over the governance of the club. This was not, as with Houlding's new venture, a business proposition. Indeed, Everton chairman George Mahon, speaking to an Everton shareholder meeting in 1895, commented that: 'The workingmen of Liverpool represented the backbone of the club'.[16]

Houlding's control over ownership of Liverpool FC gave him the ability to surround himself with trusted and like-minded people. There would be no room for anyone of a Liberal disposition in the Liverpool boardroom or amongst the shareholders, and still less for anyone holding temperance sympathies. He had had quite enough of that influence in his final years as Everton president. The club rules on the admission of new subscribers gave Houlding the means to control the social profile of Liverpool FC. 'New members shall be elected only at executive committee meetings and shall be duly proposed and seconded by two members of the executive', the club's Articles of Association determined. The men he brought into the Liverpool boardroom were in lock-step with him, socially and politically. Its very first directors and officials in 1892 were nearly all true-blue Tories. Houlding, the president of the club, was joined by two vice presidents: Benjamin E Bailey, a Conservative alderman in neighbouring Bootle, and Ephraim Walker, Conservative city councilor for West Derby. The first chairman of the club was Edwin Berry, the solicitor of the Working Men's Conservative Association and future Tory city councilor for Breckfield Ward. The eight-man committee was populated by longstanding ally, Alex Nisbet, the manager of the Bootle Conservative Club, and Thomas Howarth, William Houlding, John McKenna, and William Gunning, all four men being members of the Liverpool Constitutional Association. The club treasurer, Richard H. Webster, was a member of the St Domingo branch of the Working Men's Conservative Association. This solid connection between the Liverpool boardroom and

Conservative politics was maintained throughout—and, indeed beyond—the period the Houlding family controlled the club.

If the presence of men involved in drink-trade defence associations was a matter of controversy at Everton FC, their involvement in the Liverpool boardroom was nonproblematic. This probably accounts for the take up of shares in the new club by some of the largest breweries in the city: Bents, Tarbuck, and Threlfall brewers all owned shares in Liverpool FC. In conjunction with Houlding's own huge take up of shares it meant the club was very much a creature of the local brewing industry, as so many of the newly incorporated English and Scottish football clubs were.

What united the men who made it onto the Liverpool board was their loyalty, even debt, to John Houlding. In many cases they owed their livelihoods to him—men who worked in his brewery or who he had a hand in employing at the West Derby Union. Other men were beholden to him politically. Due to his complete control over Liverpool FC, Houlding was able to create the identity of the new football club and determine the path it would follow. Liverpool FC resembled something of a private gentleman's club. This notion gains traction when reading observations of the organisation in the local sporting press from the period. 'The shareholders of Liverpool FC', stated the *Athletic News* in May 1899, 'are a few private gentlemen, who will meet when it pleases them, and let the public know just as much of their affairs as they may choose to communicate'. Later in that year the same journal (favourably comparing the Liverpool FC annual meeting with the traditionally more rambunctious Everton FC affairs) commented: 'When the harmony of the proceedings is compared with the wild behaviour at Everton's annual meeting, it is open to question whether, from some point of view, at any rate, a private football concern is not to be preferred to a public one. Liverpool FC are not likely to invite outside subscriptions just yet. The management is composed of a few wealthy gentlemen who prefer shouldering liabilities themselves to inviting the public to share them'.[17]

THE RISE OF LIVERPOOL FOOTBALL CLUB

Setting up Liverpool FC was an expensive business. Besides the thousands of pounds spent on shares, Houlding's ambitions meant that the outlay on players would need to be sizeable if they were to quickly leap into the big time of the Football League First Division. The *Liverpool Review* reported that at least £4,000 was spent to bring established professionals to Anfield for their first season. The bulk of this was spent north of the border on Scottish professionals. Club director and head scout John McKenna made for Scotland to choose from the hundreds of good players for sale in this football hotbed, and it became an established source of talent for the club in its early years. These professionals, however, had made the decision to gamble with their careers in joining a club like Liverpool stuck for now in the lowly Lancashire League, and they needed to be tempted south by high wages. Houlding had to pay on average a whopping £300 per year wage for his 'Team of the Macs' (the soubriquet settled on for his team of Scottish football mercenaries). When the maximum weekly wage was established eight years later by the game's authorities, it would be set at £4 per week. In 1892, Houlding's enticement to his new players netted them almost £6 per week—such was the risk they were taking to join his lowly, if ambitious, outfit. On top of the fees paid to other clubs who owned the registration of these players, Houlding would have seen an outlay of about £5,000 in his first summer spending—overshooting the reported budget by a thousand pounds.

But the desired objective of First Division football meant also a stadium fit for purpose, and Houlding knew that the departure of Everton— along with the removable parts of the Anfield Stadium (including stands and turnstiles)—had left the club's ground in no fit state for spectators of the top-flight English game. His cash was called upon again, therefore, to upgrade Anfield. Having settled matters with near neighbor John Orrell over the purchase of his adjoining land, the decision was made to rebuild all stands around the pitch and to add a new grandstand; this brought the stadium capacity up to between twenty-five thousand and thirty thousand. But John Houlding would have nodded in quiet satisfaction in 1894 at the glowing review Anfield received from the *Liverpool Mercury*: 'It may be safely stated that the directors of the two leading local clubs have shown an enterprise and go ahead persistently worthy of all praise as having placed the seaport city in possession of undoubtedly the two finest grounds in the country'.[18]

Even more of a delight was the progress his team were making under the direction of the former Everton secretary and long-time ally William Barclay. Liverpool had hit the ground running. The 1892–1893 season saw them make short work of regional opposition in the Lancashire League—as one might expect of professionals playing against inferior opposition. Only eight points were dropped in the twenty-two-game season, as Liverpool topped the league. Attendances, though, were disappointing, to say the least; less than a thousand fans were attracted to Anfield for each home game in the vast majority of cases. After an easy 7-1 victory, the *Liverpool Mercury*'s match reporter commented: 'They are too clever for their opponents at present; but surely such a combination is not to "waste its sweetness on the desert air". The Liverpool public was represented by only three hundred on Saturday. This is regrettable'.[19] No matter, the Lancashire League opposition had served their purpose and John Houlding had his first silverware, and the first installment back on his huge investment. As enjoyable as that was, Liverpool that same season also reached the Liverpool Senior Cup Final—and defeated Everton. The game, played in front of a crowd of ten thousand people at nearby Bootle FCs Hawthorne Road ground on 23 April 1893, was won by a solitary goal by Liverpool to seal victory in the first-ever Liverpool derby; and, adding insult to injury, that goal was scored by ex-Everton player Tom Wylie. The success was perhaps sweeter still because Everton refused to accept the defeat, complaining that the referee had failed to award a late penalty in their favour. The trophy presentation had to be abandoned because of Everton's complaints. However, after the Liverpool FA dismissed the Everton case for a rematch, the trophy was finally handed to Liverpool a month later and paraded on a night of celebration at Liverpool's club headquarters, the Sandon Hotel. On the same night, the Lancashire League trophy was also handed over to Houlding.

As one might imagine, the mood was joyous, and Houlding milked the occasion for all it was worth. After receiving the fulsome praise of the president of the Lancashire Football Association ('You have the finest team in the league, the finest ground and headquarters, and the finest president'), Houlding was prompted to reply by the banging of pipes and glasses on tables. After thanking his V.I.P. guests for their attendance he reminded all those assembled that 'Although my committee work under a new name, this club is managed by the same men who have made football in Liverpool—the game was fostered under our care. Our club that we oversee has grown and expanded at break-neck speed, despite the efforts of some within the city to scupper it and ruin me as a person'.[20] This was vintage Houlding: scoring points against his detractors at every turn—

positioning his new club as continuity with the past and, by implication, the relocated Everton FC as the upstart new entity on the city's football scene. The speech also played on a familiar Houlding riff—that of a man facing countless obstacles placed in his path by others seeking to do him down. Away from football, there was more cause for celebration for John Houlding that spring when his only son, William, was married. As his daughter Alice-Margaret had done, William married into a commercially successful family of Tory stock. His bride was Henrietta Tinsley, the daughter of former Conservative mayor of Dudley, Thomas Henry Tinsley, the owner of chain-making workshops in the West Midlands. In the space of two generations the Houldings—a practically penniless family of farm labourers from west Lancashire—had established themselves in the commercial elite.

The following season the club—with dues paid as far as the Football League were concerned—were invited to play in English football's second tier: League Division Two. If there were any concerns about the step up in class, there need not have been. Liverpool went the whole twenty-eight game season unbeaten to top the league, dropping just six points along the way. They then won the two-legged 'challenge test' played at Blackburn Rovers' ground against the last-place team in the First Division, Mancunian team Newton Heath, to gain promotion to the English First Division. The Herculean effort to reassemble a top-flight football team at Anfield was, in two years, complete. It was a remarkable accomplishment. The *Liverpool Review* captured the scene of the returning heroes from Blackburn: 'On arriving from Tithebarn Street station the team was met by an enormously big and enthusiastic crowd. Different players were carried shoulder high to their special conveyance and after lubrication at the Alexandra Hotel the men drove off to the Sandon where another tremendous reception awaited them. The team have done wonders; so, indeed, have the committee and officers of the club'.[21] One face missing amongst the celebrants, however, was the president himself. Houlding had left the country in March for a two-month tour of the Holy Land on city council business, missing the final encounters of the league season and playoff games. This decision underlined the supreme faith he placed in his secretary-coach, William Barclay, and in John McKenna, a director who coordinated team affairs in a way which perhaps in today's football industry would earn him the title of director of football or sporting director.

In 1892, the odds on Houlding's club matching Everton FC on and off the pitch in the space of two years were huge. The new club back in 1892 had a stadium picked almost bare of quality infrastructure, just one or two loyal players who had remained at Anfield, and with no reputation whatsoever in local football circles, much less in the wider world of football. To catch up to Everton and become an elite English club playing their football in one of the more superior stadiums that English club football had to offer underlines the drive and determination of a man like John Houlding to overcome the odds. However, the speed at which this feat was achieved added fuel to the fire of the already bitter relationship existing between the two clubs. Confrontation with Everton was one of the hallmarks of the Houlding period at Liverpool. It was perhaps fanciful to believe—with everything that had happened in the old club between extremely hostile factions—that Everton and Liverpool could peacefully inhabit the same space. This was the fervent wish of the local press which wondered out loud on many an occasion why they could not just 'bury the hatchet', but it was never likely to happen. For those running the two clubs, hostilities ceased only briefly with the death of men who had served each club as committeemen and directors—though even on these occasions cordiality was usually marked by a floral tribute sent to the bereaved family on behalf of their clubs.

The bad blood flowed in both directions, though it has to be said that the episodic outbursts of John Houlding (no doubt still seething from his toppling from Everton) were a major contribution to this state of affairs. In the immediate aftermath of the separation of Everton FC from Anfield, Houlding had made it nigh on impossible for the departing club to remove certain items which they legally owned from the stadium to their new ground—an obstruction requiring legal action by Everton FC in order to retrieve their property.[22] And for years after the split with Everton, Houlding persistently made reference in public to the dispute that ended his reign as being politically motivated. His actions against his former club on occasion could descend into spite. For instance, twice Everton FC attempted to reopen relations with Stanley Hospital—historically, and initially through the club's association with John Houlding—Everton FC's official beneficiary of charitable donations. Everton approached Liverpool FC to suggest a charity match to be held at each club's grounds on alternate years to raise cash for Stanley Hospital. The Liverpool Committee declined, determined to keep the charity their own.

Shortly after the snub, Everton organised a lottery draw to be held at Goodison Park with the proceeds to be donated to Stanley Hospital. However, the lottery came to the attention of the public prosecutor's office which declared it 'an illegal act, subject to heavy penalty'.[23] William Clayton of the Everton board declared, 'Some person has made it his business to communicate with the public prosecutor informing them of the selling of lottery tickets. Who the person is who has taken this action we cannot say, but we can safely affirm that it is no supporter of the Everton Football Club. We strongly urge the public to show their disgust at this action'.[24] Almost certainly the complaint came from the Liverpool FC Committee, and in all likelihood from John Houlding himself.

From press coverage though, one senses that these acts may have been encouraged if not provoked by the rather superior attitude the Everton hierarchy took towards Liverpool. For the most part, the Everton men were from the professional classes (doctors, accountants, solicitors, and the like) who would—in addition to their longstanding antipathy towards John Houlding and his allies from the old club—have looked down on men of commerce, or more accurately put: men of commerce seeking to profit from their association with a sporting organisation. The *Liverpool Review* scolded the Everton board for what it saw as their lofty pretensions. 'How contemptible is the attitude which the Everton people are taking in regard to Liverpool—an attitude so unsporting that no amount of argument or sophistry can explain it away . . . The Everton officials should remember that the hallmark of a gentleman lies in the fact that he even treats his supposed inferiors with respect'.[25] The hostilities between the leadership of both clubs were also matched on the terraces. Again, it was the *Liverpool Review* to the fore, and again they highlighted the apparent prejudices of the Evertonians towards their Liverpool counterparts. In 1894, the *Review*'s report on an Everton game seemed more concerned with the Goodison faithful's 'Grim spirit of antagonism' towards Liverpool FC, as news came through to the ground that their neighbours were losing a match away at Port Vale. And again, in January 1895, when Liverpool were struggling to survive in the Football League First Division, their victory away at Burnley was loudly booed, prompting the *Review*'s reporter to declare 'Such "sports" as these are beneath our notice. They believe in one team only. "Biased spirits". Jeering and crying down Liverpool is not only paltry, it is sickening'.[26] For purposes of balance it should be said that sportsmanship and bias in local rivalries are seldom one-sided. Nevertheless, its manifestation does underline the depth of hostility between the two clubs, and how close John Houlding's new club were to becoming an established force in the city capable of threatening Everton's supremacy.

There were, of course, teething troubles for Liverpool. Their rapid ascent to the top-flight was on the strength of what was, in essence, a functional team of solid professionals with only one or two players who would have been considered talented enough for the elite clubs in the division. Relegation in 1895 after just one season in the First Division gave the Liverpool board pause for thought, and the conclusion they reached was that they needed sweeping changes in personnel, and not only amongst the playing squad. Club secretary William Barclay had done more than a reasonable job as, effectively, team manager. However, in 1896, after gaining promotion again to the top-flight, Liverpool's professionalism received a massive boost when Sunderland's Tom Watson—the English game's first superstar manager, having won three of the previous four season's league titles with Sunderland—was head-hunted by Houlding and brought to Anfield. In an era when club committees still prevailed concerning the choice of matchday starting lineups and determining which players would be bought and sold, Watson was a pioneer in insisting that all playing and financial matters were his territory. He was also media savvy—a charismatic leader who knew what to say in order to boost the club's profile and manage expectations. A man with the organisational skills of Watson was worth the £300 per year salary Houlding paid him. Without a doubt, Houlding would have recognised the Newcastle-born manager as a fellow alpha male who could take care of the playing side of the club as he took care of its overall governance. And this he duly did. In his first three seasons at Liverpool he took the club to fifth, ninth, and runners-up positions, and reached two semifinals of the FA Cup in the same period. By the turn of the new century, Houlding's Liverpool were a truly top competitive outfit. Under the guidance of Tom Watson, they were realistically in the hunt for both league and cup glory.

* * *

With the creation of Liverpool FC, John Houlding had not only transformed the sporting (indeed cultural) life of the city, he had also helped to successfully reinvent himself. Though still well regarded as an important figure in the Tory Party in Liverpool, by the early 1890s his chances of advancing to the party leadership or becoming an MP had been checked.

The setting up of Liverpool FC—though forced on him—had proven to be a decisive shift in fortunes for him. Free of the sniping comments of his Everton detractors, Houlding was able to recast himself as a benefactor; someone associated with the building up of an important public institution rather than as a man exploiting and undermining one. Little did he know the historical consequences of his achievement in founding Liverpool FC: a club that would go on to dominate English football and become a global 'brand' for millions. In this respect, his son William's words were prophetic. When addressing the assembled squad of the club's original players in the summer of 1892, the younger Houlding predicted that 'This team the committee has got together will give the lie to those who say we will only have a park team, and will have to play only park teams. We of Liverpool Football Club intend to make ourselves felt in the world of football'.[27]

By the mid-1890s, all was well in the world of football, but outside of it, John Houlding was far from finished making his mark. The foundation of Liverpool FC proved to be a springboard for a number of late triumphs in his life.

6

JOHN HOULDING,
LORD MAYOR OF LIVERPOOL

In the 1890s, male life expectancy in England was less than forty-five years, so John Houlding, in his early sixties, was a man already into his old age by the mortality standards of the day. He was also beset by longstanding ill health—a bitter blow for someone who had always prided himself on his vitality and physique. A bronchial condition dogged him and prevented him from attending to his normal public duties and workload, and his bouts of ill health were becoming more persistent. There is a definite sense of a gearing down in Houlding's life over the course of the 1890s—a sense that he would choose causes and involve himself in them more judiciously. Nowhere was this more so than in his political life. Analysis of the local press—which covered the city's political scene comprehensively—suggests a reduced involvement in Conservative circles. Though this observation is relative to Houlding's earlier extensive involvement in politics, there is a discernible retreat away from frontline politics. It is true that he maintained his positions as a councillor and chairman of the Everton Divisional Council, but he is noticeably absent from the thick of the action at the top of the party, and it would appear that most of his major political battles were behind him at this stage. This winding down can partly be explained by Houlding's parliamentary ambitions having been thwarted. That was, as noted already, his long-held ambition, and the denial of it would naturally result in his taking a step back from a central role in the party. Another important factor was the changing tone and tenor of Liverpool Conservative politics.

As we have seen, by the early 1890s the Liverpool Conservative Party was consumed by an ideological civil war between a pragmatic leadership, whose chief concern was the return of Conservative MPs from the city to parliament, and those preoccupied by religious affairs, like the powerful Working Men's Conservative Association, which insisted on making Protestantism the leitmotif of Liverpool Conservatism. The struggle between these two opposing forces consumed the party in the final decade of the nineteenth century. In districts like Everton and Kirkdale—Houlding's fiefdom—a new brand of ward representative had come to the fore. Men like evangelical firebrand preacher Austin Taylor, who took a council seat in Everton and would go on to represent East Toxteth in parliament, were now the face of the Tory Party in Liverpool. John Houlding was no stranger to politics that appealed to the Protestant working class, but this appeal was on the basis of an affirmation of the Union with Ireland and the profession of his loyalty to Crown and empire. Though an Orangeman himself, the more naked sectarian political pitch of the new breed of Conservative activists was alien to him. Houlding's style was that of a populist; a benevolent boss politician who used his larger-than-life personality to appeal to anyone who could be persuaded away from radical politics to back Tory Democracy. The buttressing of Protestantism from the perceived advance of 'ritualism' within the Church of England and checking 'the growing demands' of Roman Catholics was not Houlding's theme. He was a common-sense politician, not an ideologue. But the party was moving in that ideological direction. Political leadership was now measured by how committed one was to narrow-minded religious bigotry, and Houlding was increasingly a man out of his time.

In any case, factional fighting and ideological purity were too energy-sapping and time consuming for a man in Houlding's condition. In light of this, the conferment upon him in 1895 of the status of city alderman was a welcome development. Becoming alderman meant that Houlding would only be required to contest his council seat every six years, so his need to engage with the electorate and pander to the new evangelical political creed for electoral purposes was not an issue he had to contend with. Also, his old (and huge) council seat of Everton and Kirkdale had finally been broken up into four council wards: Breckfield, Everton, St

Domingo, and Netherfield, after the passing of the Local Government Act of 1894 had standardised the size of council wards. Houlding now represented a much smaller population in the newly created St Domingo ward; what's more, he was able to bring his influence to bear in Everton on who would contest two of the other three new wards in the district. His fellow Liverpool FC directors, Edwin Berry and Simon Jude, were the beneficiaries of this authority and were a shoo-in for the Breckfield and Netherfield wards, respectively.

By this time Houlding's commitment to his business empire had also tapered off. His brewery was being run by John James Ramsey and his son, William, while John McKenna was largely in control of the day-to-day running of Liverpool FC. This afforded him more time to attend to other matters. Family was important to him, but perhaps, like many driven men, it was a neglected part of his life. Houlding was the patriarch to an extended family. In 1894, there had been another addition to it when son William and his wife Henrietta made him and his wife Jane grandparents for the third time with the birth of their daughter, Audrey Houlding. This extended family became even more important to John when on the 1 November 1896 his wife Jane died after a long illness at the age of seventy-two.

John and Jane had been married for forty years and the loss, no matter how well presaged, must have been an enormous blow to John. Mrs Houlding had made the journey with her husband from his time as head brewer at Clarkson's Brewery. It is difficult, in lieu of solid information, not to sound dismissive about the wife of a larger-than-life Victorian man. Such women can often and unfairly become the anonymous footnotes in their husband's story. The *Liverpool Courier* tribute to Jane Houlding, however, gives us at least some flavour of her character. 'Quiet and unobtrusive in manner, Mrs Houlding while in health delighted in kindly deeds among the poor, and every philanthropic movement in Everton obtained from her willing aid. She was much esteemed by the neighbours among whom she had lived so long, and the greatest sympathy will be felt for Mr Houlding and his family in the sad bereavement they have sustained'.[1] Amongst the mourners at her funeral were representatives of the playing staff of Liverpool FC and its board of directors; a floral tribute was also sent by Everton FC. (This gesture from Everton was a mark of respect for Mrs Houlding and condolence for her husband. But the long-hoped-for thaw between the two organisations was still some way off.)

His wife's death must have brought into sharper focus Houlding's own mortality. He was himself, after all, beset by long-standing ill health. Frequently in the last decade of his life he would leave the smoggy city and head off to sunnier and cleaner environs to convalesce. As a French speaker, Houlding liked to visit the South of France. Nice, on the French Riviera, was his favourite destination and, in particular, the resort of Cimiez. Cimiez, a Roman spa town, must have been a draw to Houlding for its water's purported healing and rejuvenating qualities. With its *belle epoque* architecture, the resort was an exclusive destination for wealthy European families to migrate to in the winter. It thus appealed to Houlding's sense of grandeur. That Cimiez was the favourite retreat of Queen Victoria, who took up frequent residence there at the resort's Exelsior Regina Palace, would also have pleased the fervent monarchist.

Houlding's trips abroad, though, often combined business with pleasure. As chair of the Liverpool Brewers and Wine Spirits Merchants Association, Houlding visited the wine-producing regions of France, especially Bordeaux, in an effort to open up new suppliers for his members. On one such occasion, in 1895, he travelled with Thomas McCracken, his old political friend, and himself a wine spirits dealer. McCracken, feeling the need to keep the citizens of Liverpool abreast of their activities corresponded with the *Liverpool Mercury* about the progress of their journey. 'We were particularly interested in the vine fields of Chateau Latour and were permitted to sample all their celebrated vintages. Amongst those we tasted were Chateau Haut Brion 1889; Chateau Mouton Rothschild 1872; and Chateau Palmer 1868—Chateau Palmer being a great favourite of Alderman Houlding. "King John" and myself are about to leave for Royau, which is a beautiful watering place on the coast, at the entrance to the Gironde, and only a few miles from where the Pacific steamer calls about next Tuesday when we take our departures for old England'.[2] Houlding was doubtlessly won over by Bordeaux and its fine wines: returning there twice in the following three years and extending one of these visits into Switzerland on Liverpool Brewers and Wine Spirits Merchants Association business. He was, of course, a seasoned traveller. Council business, in particular, took him far and wide to places such as Canada, Australia, and even Russia, attending a conference in Moscow on behalf of the Liverpool Council Health Committee. These later and frequent European jaunts underline that, though his powers were waning, Houlding was still a man capable of taking what life had to offer.

Indeed, his travels allowed him to add another string to his bow. After his trip to Palestine in February 1897, Houlding was booked for a series of nightly lectures at the Picton Lecture Hall, Liverpool. The Picton Hall was a 1,200-seat amphitheatre nestled between the neoclassical buildings of the Walker Art Gallery and city museum. The lecture series was entitled 'From Liverpool to Palestine', and each performance was reportedly well attended. A *Liverpool Mercury* review described one performance: 'The hall was crowded. Alderman Houlding gave a graphic account of his recent tour overland to the East, referring to the improved methods of travel in the present day as compared with some forty years ago, and described the places he visited and the objects of interest that came under his notice. The lecture, which was illustrated by lantern slide views, was attentively listened to by the audience'.[3] One can imagine the imposing figure of John Houlding pacing the stage and taking great pride as a committed imperialist in highlighting what he saw as the great civilising benefits British rule had brought to the Middle East. And perhaps Houlding regaled his audience with one other intriguing story about his trip to the East. His journey to Palestine took him to Constantinople where he was granted an audience with Sultan Hamid II, the king of the Ottoman Empire. After his meeting, Houlding was decorated by the sultan with the Order of the Imtiyaz—the highest order of merit—bestowed on Houlding for 'services rendered to the Kingdom'.[4] Quite what that service was is not entirely clear.

Houlding's sense of civic duty continued to burn brightly. He maintained his decades' association with the West Derby Union as its chairman and attended conferences up and down the country on its behalf; and Stanley Hospital continued to be the beneficiary of his time and finances—the hospital's charitable connection to Liverpool FC continued to be a welcome source of funding for the infirmary. Accepting a lifetime achievement award from the hospital's committee for his services, Houlding declared that 'It has always been my endeavour to serve the interests of Stanley Hospital, as it is doing such good charitable work among the poorer classes of the north end'.[5] Houlding also retained his presidency of the Mersey Quay and Railway Carters' Union, taking the lead well into the late 1890s in negotiating settlements between workers and their employers. And in 1896, quite late on in life at the age of sixty-four, Houlding made another time-consuming commitment to public service by accepting the position of justice of the peace. This kept him busy hearing a multitude of cases concerning petty crimes and passing custodial sentences down when necessary. This was a position in 'respectable society' that no doubt many of his detractors believed him to be less than worthy of, given his drink trade and public house connections. But if these critics were agitated by Houlding's ascendency to the magistrate's bench, they were incandescent with rage at the next chapter in his public life: in 1897, John Houlding became Liverpool's lord mayor.

THE MAYORALTY CONTROVERSY

There was an element of the accidental about Houlding taking up the Liverpool mayoralty. The position in 1897 was due to go to the alderman for West Derby, William Bartlett. However, illness prevented Bartlett from taking up the role, and Houlding's seniority in the council chamber as an alderman with over a decade of service as a councillor and alderman, and who had travelled the world on council business, made him the most obvious replacement. There had been talk of Houlding becoming lord mayor from the time he had been denied both the Everton and the Kirkdale parliamentary candidacies. The position was a highly prestigious one at the time: it had been the preserve of shipping merchants such as Sir William Bowring and Robert Durning Holt, and local aristocratic landowners such as the Earl of Derby. Becoming lord mayor would be a significant consolation to losing out on being elected as a member of parliament. Regardless of this long-trailed association with the position, when his name was pushed to the fore as the likely nominee it unleashed a storm of protest. As always with John Houlding, everything he got was hard fought for.

The political clout that temperance groups had in Liverpool had not weakened in the period since Houlding had last taken them on half a decade earlier when they had attempted to unseat him from the council chamber and all but scuppered his parliamentary hopes. The very name 'Houlding' was as a red rag to a bull amongst the temperance advocates. Arrayed against him, and determined to stop the ratification of his nomination for lord mayor, were a variety of church abstinence and temperance societies, the Liberal Party (inevitably), and even some temperance-minded Conservatives. The local Liberal-leaning press were also determined to poison the well for Houlding. In late September of 1897, an organisation called the Liverpool Teetotal Crusade met at Temperance Hall in the city centre to coordinate their response to Houlding's nomination. An uncompromising and hard-hitting statement was the result of the meeting: 'One matter we intend to fight to the end—we are not going to have a liquor man for the Lord Mayor of Liverpool. The Liquor traffic stands for everything that is vile in national life'.[6]

As before, the temperance movement were quite prepared to personalise the issue and call into question Houlding's moral suitability for a high-profile public position. The Reverend B. Veitch of the Congregational Crescent Chapel, a proponent of the social gospel and, in politics, a Liberal, elaborated on the subject: 'Certain good people who would wish to find apologists for this try to distinguish between the alderman as a kindly good fellow and philanthropist, as they view him, and the alderman as a brewer and publican. [But] the would-be philanthropist who is a brewer must share responsibility for the results of his trade'.[7] The Great George Street Chapel Brotherhood condemned the Tory Party's decision to nominate Houlding by stating that 'To elect a representative of the liquor trade to the office of Chief Magistrate [Lord Mayor] would be to associate the highest dignity of the city with a trade whose prosperity means suffering, poverty, vice and crime to many citizens'.[8] And this theme of civic shame was taken up by the Reverend Charles Aked—the leading temperance voice in the city at this time: 'People could not help but be ashamed that a man involved in a devilish and destructive trade [can be] elevated to the Lord Mayor of Liverpool . . . Liverpool would become contemptable in the eyes of the great cities of England. The second city of the empire has fallen to the level of Wigan, and like that cursed town has found its chief magistrate in a publican'.[9] Not only was this a denigration of Houlding's trade, but using the word 'publican' to describe him was also a calculated insult to his status as a significant employer in Liverpool, not to mention to his standing as an alderman and magistrate.

The Tory hierarchy, though—and unlike when Houlding was left exposed earlier in the decade—came out fighting for their man. Denouncing the attacks on their choice for lord mayor as needlessly impugning what they described as Houlding's 'calling', they rounded on the Reverend Aked, in particular; dismissing him as 'an impudent young man' and a 'clerical ruffian', and chiding that his name 'would be forgotten whilst the name of Mr Houlding would be well remembered'.[10] Unrepentant, though, the Reverend Aked countered: 'I denounce most emphatically the appointment of Alderman Houlding as Chief Magistrate of the city. The question was not of party politics, but one in which we, as a United Free Church Council, had a right to express an opinion and to protest against any member of the brewer fraternity holding such a position as Chief Magistrate of the City of Liverpool'.[11]

A raging civic debate over Houlding's nomination for lord mayor took place throughout September and October of 1897, and the Liberal Party sought to take full advantage of it in the municipal election campaign of that autumn. For the Liberals, Houlding's proposed mayoralty was further proof, if any more were needed, of the drink trade's control of Liverpool life under Conservative rule. One Liberal critic of John Houlding who he knew very well was temperance fanatic Dr William Whitford. A scourge of Houlding on the Everton FC Committee prior to the 1892 split, Whitford, a justice of the peace, had also raised objections to Houlding becoming a justice of the peace a year earlier. Whitford reasoned then that it was preposterous that Houlding could become a magistrate given that much of the magistrate's rulings would be on the granting of public house licences and other regulatory matters concerning the drink trade. The Irishman's constant attacks on his fellow magistrates sitting on the licensing bench earned him the nickname from the *Liverpool Review*: the Hibernian Whip. Predictably, Whitford was a fierce critic of Houlding's nomination to become chief magistrate. However, and ironically, one of the reasons Houlding may have become lord mayor was that Whitford had managed to defame the man with the power to push through a mayoral nomination: Liverpool's Tory Party supremo, Sir Arthur Bower Forwood.

Whitford had publicly accused Forwood—himself a magistrate—of pushing through a raft of liquor license applications, despite the reservations of fellow magistrates. He basically accused Forwood of doing the bidding of the major brewers in Liverpool who relied on their tied houses acquiring licenses in order to trade. The combative Forwood's wrath was immediate, accusing Whitford of 'fanatical partisanship' and holding a 'warped judgement' which had cast doubt on his [Forwood's] objectivity as a magistrate. He demanded a retraction from Whitford, a man he considered to be 'the mouthpiece of the Radical Party in Liverpool'.

Forwood's colleague, Archibald Salvidge, chairman of the Liverpool Working Men's Conservative Association (and, as mentioned, managing director of Bents Brewery), joined in the attack on Whitford, describing him as 'unfit for public life, and unfit for the position of Justice of the Peace in the city'.[12] But no apology was forthcoming from Whitford. It was in the wake of this well-publicised spat that Alderman Bartlett withdrew his nomination for the lord mayoralty and the name of Whitford's arch enemy in the district of Everton (and Everton FC), John Houlding, was put forward in its stead. Coincidence? Perhaps, but Forwood was not a man to cross, especially in such a public manner. It is entirely possible, therefore, that a man who had been instrumental in taking away from Houlding the control of one civic institution, Everton FC, was inadvertently responsible for him gaining the prestigious office of the lord mayoralty of Liverpool. Unintended consequences indeed. From incidents like this it is easy to understand how the bad blood that existed between the leaders of Everton and Liverpool football clubs persisted for years after the split of 1892.

At a council Select Committee on 26 October 1897 chaired by Arthur Forwood, John Houlding's name alone was considered for the lord mayoralty and settled upon. The decision was relayed via a statement to the press: 'Alderman John Houlding has been chosen as a fit and proper person for the lord mayoralty of Liverpool for the coming municipal year. This pays him a high compliment for the zeal, ability and self-sacrificing spirit he has displayed in connection with his work for the good of the general community'.[13] It was a statement the council's Select Committee knew would inflame opinion in some quarters. Houlding's confirmation as new lord mayor certainly did nothing to take the wind out of the sails of his sternest critics. A special meeting of the Executive Committee of the Church of England Temperance Society issued a statement deploring the decision: 'We have heard with extreme regret of the nomination of a brewer to the Lord Mayoralty of Liverpool. Whilst not in any way impugning the private character of the nominee, we believe that such an appointment would be distasteful to the Christian conscience of the community. We consider the association of the Chief Magistracy with the drink interest to be detrimental to the true welfare of the city'.[14] Predictably, the Reverend Charles Aked had his say on the final decision to endorse Houlding. If it was now a fait accompli that he was to be sworn in as lord mayor, Aked urged a boycott on his year in office: 'I hope all charitable and philanthropic agencies of the city will never disgrace themselves by allowing a liquor seller to preside over their annual meetings'.[15]

However, Houlding's selection was not met by universal opposition. Far from it. There occurred something of a backlash against the priggish criticism he had received. By and large the Tory Party backed Houlding, save for those who took up a temperance stance. And with their refusal to oppose Houlding, so too did the traditional foes of the Conservatives in Liverpool, the Irish National League. Though normally aligned with the Liberal Party on matters of high politics (particularly over Irish Home Rule), the city's Irish politicians parted company with them on many social issues. One such issue was temperance reform. The Irish National League president, Councillor George Lynskey, gave his group's response to the Houlding selection: 'This party, while following the usual course of not supporting the nominee of the Tories for the Lord Mayoralty, nevertheless resolves to offer no opposition to the election of Alderman John Houlding to the Chief Magistracy of the city'.[16] Another group calling itself the National Liberty Defence Association went further: 'We heartily congratulate Alderman Houlding on his triumphant success by being chosen as the Lord Mayor of this great city, knowing him to be a gentleman who will occupy the position with great dignity, honour and respect'.[17] Letters to the press from individuals offering their support to the Houlding selection underlines a sense that his more vocal opponents had overstepped the mark. One correspondent to the *Liverpool Mercury* stated, 'I feel bound to protest against some of the language used with respect to Alderman Houlding, as it is in accordance with neither fairness nor reason. It strikes me as hitting below the belt to reproach Mr Houlding for his private calling'. Another irate letter writer condemned the hypocrisy of certain churchmen who criticised Houlding's trade while accepting 'pew rents' and subscriptions from 'the Whitley's, the Greenall's, and others who own pubs and brew beer'. One letter in support of Houlding detected the whiff of class bias mixed into the criticism of him: 'Mr Houlding may not have the advantage of high scholastic education [but] he has raised himself from a humble position with honour'.[18]

It is fair to say that Houlding's journey to the Town Hall for his investiture on 9 November 1897 had been down a rocky road. And his opponents were still intent yet on marring the ceremony itself. The Liberal Party as a bloc voted to stay away from the mayoral swearing-in ceremony; only Conservative and Irish Nationalist councillors took their places at noon in the council chamber. If Houlding felt any embarrassment at this snub, his discomfort would have been deepened by his first responsibility as the new lord mayor: to read out a representative sample of letters from individuals and organisations concerning the choice of chief magistrate. Usually a formality of backslapping and well-wishing, in 1897 it inevitably meant that Houlding would have to stand and read out a series of critical missives aimed at him. It is not difficult to imagine that this was a humiliating ordeal. No matter how thick skinned and battle hardened John Houlding was, acknowledging that a sizable number of church and secular groups thought his advance to the position of lord mayor was 'detrimental' to the welfare of the city must have been a difficult moment for him to get through. When this task was complete, however, the tone of the proceedings changed markedly.

Conservative leader Arthur Forwood rose to his feet and launched a stinging rebuke against those dissenting against the new lord mayor. To the obvious relief and approval of the Conservative-dominated council chamber, Forwood declared: 'The documents read out here today were to the effect that, no matter what a man's character might be—provided his trade was not one in consonance with the views of the gentlemen whose communications had been read out—the public ought not give any recognition to the services rendered by the gentleman. I consider this to be a pharisaic attempt on the part of a number of people in this town and it will be condemned by the citizens of it'.[19]

Turning towards more pleasant matters, Forwood revealed that Houlding had written a letter to him expressing his desire to imitate the example of the old mayor of London, Dick Whittington, and become lord mayor of Liverpool. Houlding had written to the Select Committee that he hoped and believed that they would confer upon him that distinction, and in doing so they would be indicating to every schoolboy in Liverpool that there was a possibility of reaching the highest position in their city.[20] The story was a disarming one, and its air of naivety contrasted favourably with the aggressive and negative campaign launched against Houlding— which is no doubt why Forwood repeated it. But the retelling of it also revealed how much Houlding was willing to trade on his personal rags-to-riches story.

Finally on the day of the investiture, Houlding himself rose to speak about what the mayoralty meant to him. 'Gentlemen, I thank you sincerely for the honour this day you have conferred upon me by electing me to the high and distinguished position of Lord Mayor of my native city. To be chosen for that office in such a city as Liverpool, the first seaport of the world, is an honour which any man would feel proud. It would be mere affectation on my part if I did not express what I sincerely feel, that this is the proudest day of my life'.[21] This last sentence gained huge applause in the chamber.

Not without a fight, Houlding had secured one of the greatest honours in Liverpool public life. Indeed, given Liverpool's status as one of the great metropolises, his name would become known nationally and internationally. And despite the gloomy prognostications of the naysayers who had predicted shame and notoriety, John Houlding's tenure as lord mayor was almost universally considered a great success. He threw himself into the role with gusto, attending a huge number of events, organising and paying from his own pocket a good proportion of them, and was clearly determined to make his mayoralty one to remember. Typical of the man, the great office he had taken up was made to showcase *his* talents and to promote *his* image. Attending the annual Cow Keeper's Association show, Houlding advised his audience: 'The Association might congratulate itself upon having as its president the Lord Mayor of the city, and one who had early association with your trade'—Houlding's career trajectory being underlined by this (no doubt tongue-in-cheek) commentary. To be fair to Houlding, however, his own self-promotion went hand in hand with using the mayoralty to project many of the civic causes he had a long association with: the well-being of the poor, advocacy for better sanitation in the city, and the plight of orphaned and destitute children. And Houlding remembered his own family roots while in office. His family, as we know, hailed from Heskin in rural West Lancashire, and his sympathies were on display when a nearby mining community, Tawd Vale, was wiped out. A Town Hall fund was set up by Houlding to alleviate the hardship of the families left destitute by the loss of their income, and Houlding also visited the site to pay his respects.

After his year in office had elapsed, Liverpool's principal society journal, *The Porcupine*, published a celebratory ode to Houlding's contribution to the city while lord mayor:

> A year of splendid work most nobly done,
> A year of usefulness to rich and poor,
> A year of honours great, but fairly won,

A 'record year', whose memory shall endure.
Detractors now are silenced, one and all,
Straightforwardness and truth have gained the day,
One universal tribute comes from great and small.
'Well done, John Houlding', are the words they say,
Take back to private life the hearty thanks,
Of all to whom a good example set,
Who wish to rise above the common ranks,
And feel they may be something better yet. [22]

Leaving aside the rather grand claims regarding the inspirational merits of Houlding's term of office, the compliment does convey his perfect execution of his responsibilities to the city as lord mayor. His time in the position certainly relaunched him as a prominent political figure. When the sitting MP for Kirkdale, George Baden Powell, died shortly after Houlding's mayoralty ended, he was again being talked about as a possible replacement. However, such notions were not to be entertained by the man himself. Houlding stuck to his word from five years earlier that age and health issues were too great an impediment to him taking up a place at Westminster.

FREEMASONRY: HOULDING ELECTED TO THE GRAND LODGE COUNCIL OF ENGLAND

One national role Houlding did take up willingly, however, was a place on the Grand Lodge Council of England, freemasonry's ruling body. This was an elevation which brought John Houlding into the company of the country's elite; an honour which, along with the Liverpool mayoralty, ensured a satisfying end to his years of striving for local and national recognition. Freemasonry has only briefly been touched on so far, but it played a huge part in Houlding's life.

John Houlding's introduction to freemasonry came in 1871 when, as a man who owned his own brewery, he was initiated into Everton Lodge. Freemasonry has a pyramid structure with multiple levels, so unsurprisingly Houlding was determined to rise through the ranks of 'the Craft'. By 1877 he had reached the position of Worshipful Master of his mother lodge (effectively its leader) and in that same year founded Anfield Lodge. In subsequent years, he would go on to found Walton Lodge and

Sir Walter Raleigh Lodge; the latter in conjunction with Sir John Willox, the proprietor of the *Liverpool Courier* and MP for Everton. Houlding's Sandon Hotel became the *de facto* home to a network of lodges in north Liverpool who held their meetings there. (The Sandon was decorated with tiles bearing masonic symbolism on both its interior and exterior— still visible now on the pub's exterior.) In the 1880s, Houlding advanced to regional honours in freemasonry, gaining the positions of Provincial Grand Warden and Provincial Grand Registrar of West Lancashire. When on 18 April 1898 he was sworn in as grand senior deacon of England at Grand Lodge, London, it marked the culmination of his long dedication to freemasonry. Having committed himself to learning the rites and passages of freemasonry over the course of three decades, Houlding had attained the 33rd Degree, bestowed on masons who have carried out meritorious service to craft masonry. Houlding was now a master mason—the highest possible level any mason could rise to. His peers at Grand Lodge were lords and dukes, and the grand master at the time of his investiture was Queen Victoria's eldest son, Albert Edward, the Prince of Wales. One can imagine the feeling of pride and sense of achievement this man from the most modest of backgrounds must have felt in this exclusive company.

Freemasonry also, it seems, was another activity Houlding could use to project himself. In January 1887, as part of the celebrations to mark the jubilee of Queen Victoria, the West Lancashire Province of Freemasons planned a celebratory dinner at Liverpool Town Hall. In control of the organisation of the event was John Houlding, and, in an extravagant gesture, he had struck at his own expense commemorative badges to hand to his fellow brethren gathered for the dinner. At the centre of the badge was a profile picture of Queen Victoria surmounted on the Royal Crown. Under this, on a freemasonry triangle, was the following inscription: 'John Houlding, Chairman of the West Lancashire Provincial Committee'. This was an audacious act of self-promotion, and completely consistent with his character.[23]

But freemasonry was not a pose or a pastime for Houlding, it was an institution at the centre of his existence and it consumed much of his time. It shaped his attitude and guided his actions towards business and public life; in particular, it appears to have determined who he associated closely with and how he approached the governance of the many organisations he had a significant presence in. 'I largely attribute to freemasonry', he informed a gathering of fellow freemasons at Liverpool's Masonic Hall, 'any ability I have towards the proper fulfilment of my public duties'.[24]

Probably the most telling influence freemasonry had upon Houlding was how it affected who he recruited to senior positions in the organisations he had most control over: the West Derby Union and Liverpool FC. As the chairman of the West Derby Board of Guardians for over twenty years, Houlding determined policy, direction of funds, and choice of senior employees. In respect to the latter, there was a strong overlapping connection between the two masonic lodges which were associated particularly with John Houlding—Everton Lodge and Anfield Lodge—and employment to senior professional positions of the Union. John McKenna, a vaccination officer; rate collectors, James Booth and Henry Noble; surveyor, Alexander Nisbet; registrar, Richard Webster; and relief officers William Briggs, Giles Lever, William Maddox, and Richard Maddox were members of either Everton or Anfield Lodges, and in some cases members of both. This crossover between the West Derby Union and freemasonry was underlined in a *Liverpool Mercury* report of Houlding's installation as Worshipful Master of Everton Lodge in 1877, wherein it was noted that the good wishes of 'a large representative of brethren connected with the West Derby Union, of which Brother Houlding is the chairman, were passed on to him'.[25] While not being conclusive evidence that Houlding was giving preferential treatment to his masonic brethren from Everton and Anfield lodges, there is a circumstantial case to be made that his fellow lodge members were not far away from his thoughts when recruitment to senior positions in the organisations he had a large say in were being discussed.

There was also a huge presence of freemasons within the hierarchy of Liverpool FC under John Houlding's ownership of the club. The influence of freemasons on all administrative posts at Liverpool FC was noteworthy. The positions of club president, chairman, directors, secretaries, managers, and solicitors were all dominated by freemasons, and so too was the shareholder base of the club in its first decade and a half of existence. The very first Liverpool FC annual general meeting in 1893 was overseen by a nine-man board, seven of whom were freemasons: John Houlding, chairman; Edwin Berry, treasurer; Richard H. Webster, secretary; William Barclay; and directors John McKenna, John Asbury, and John James Ramsey. Of the forty-seven original subscribers to the club in 1892 (a small number of men carefully selected by the board), twenty-one were freemasons. The number of men from Everton Lodge and Anfield Lodge involved in the administration of the club was as significant as it was amongst men employed in senior positions at the West Derby Union; twelve of the twenty-four freemasons who served as directors and other members of the club hierarchy (such as secretaries, treasurers, etc.) between 1892 and 1920 were from these two lodges.[26] The concentration of so many club officials with links to two lodges which were particularly associated with John Houlding suggests that a well-worn path between them and the Liverpool boardroom had been established in the club's earliest years.

Further to this, it should be mentioned that the Liverpool FC masonic fellowship were high-flyers in provincial freemasonry. The credentials of the club's founder, John Houlding, with regard to his status within freemasonry tends to overshadow the achievements of all other freemasons at the club. However, other men within the Liverpool hierarchy were also prominent within the Craft fraternity. It is routine to read in the biographical accounts and obituaries of these men the term 'prominent freemason'. Many were masons at more than one lodge and most had become Worshipful Masters. The involvement of club officials in freemasonry, however, went beyond the local. Besides John Houlding, seven other directors of the club were promoted to provincial rank. John James Ramsey, John McKenna, William C. Briggs, Simon Jude, and Robert Henry Webster were provincial grand deacons at West Lancashire Grand Lodge; and Albert E. Berry and his brother Edwin Berry were provincial grand deacons at Cheshire Grand Lodge. The elevation of these men within freemasonry took place under the guidance of one of the most senior freemasons in the country, who happened to sit side by side with them in the Liverpool FC boardroom.

HOULDING'S INDIAN SUMMER COMES TO AN END

Though retiring from the running of his own brewery, Houlding, approaching his seventies, was still engaged with the core institutions of his life: the Conservative Party, freemasonry, the West Derby Union, the Liverpool Brewers and Licensed Victuallers Association, and Liverpool FC. Incredibly, given his longstanding ailments, he committed even more time and energy to other causes. In 1899, he became president of the National Baseball Association. Liverpool was a stronghold of a sport more readily associated with North America. The Liverpool Baseball Association was set up in 1892 and Houlding had been a significant figure in its creation. And in 1900, the arch imperialist Houlding was keen to demonstrate his patriotism at the height of the Second Boer War. With the King's Liverpool Regiment having suffered many casualties in one of the most ferocious battles of the Boer War at the Siege of Lady-smith, Houlding helped organise, along with his son, William, the Re-servists Committee—a body set up to distribute funds to the families of Liverpool men serving in South Africa who were in financial hardship. For the same cause, Houlding later organised a 'Patriotic Demonstration' at the Picton Lecture Hall in May 1900. This was a jingoistic charity affair to raise money for servicemen's families, but also an event to support the government of the day in their prosecution of what was a very unpopular war.[27] Complete commitment to what he saw as the glory of the British Empire was Houlding's enduring philosophy.

But into the new century there were signs that all was not well with John Houlding. Battle as he might, his constant struggle against respiratory disease was taking its toll. More and more of his time was being taken up in convalescence. He spent over a month in the seaside town of Bournemouth in the spring of 1900. No sooner had he returned to Liver-pool apparently refreshed than he fell into ill health again; he left British shores for Cimiez in the South of France, hoping his favourite old haunt could help restore him to strength. Briefing their readers of their former lord mayor's health status, the *Liverpool Mercury* revealed that 'Alder-man John Houlding, who for some time past has been in indifferent health, is at present staying in Nice, and his many friends will be gratified to learn that he derives considerable benefit from his sojourn in that South of France retreat. It is understood, however, that the alderman does not propose to return to Liverpool for some weeks'.[28] It need hardly be spec-ulated upon that when in January of 1901 Queen Victoria died, a faithful subject like John Houlding would have been affected by her passing. Her death was viewed as symbolic. The Victorian Age represented the old-world order: marked by tradition and moral conservatism; the Edwardian period to come would be more free-spirited, modernist, and morally lax. A Victorian like Houlding was looking increasingly like a man out of his time.

If it was the case that Houlding felt like an anachronism, then his football team provided him with one last hurrah. In the period after Queen Victoria's death, Liverpool FC went on an unbeaten last twelve-match run in the 1900–1901 season in order to hold off a challenge from Sunderland and land the club's first major honour. Liverpool FC, formed by John Houlding less than a decade earlier, were Football League Champions of England. It had taken a huge outlay of cash in order to secure that success, but Houlding had finally taken Liverpool FC out of the shadows of Everton. The knowledge that scores had finally been settled with his rivals on the Everton board made his and Liverpool's success all the sweeter. When the victorious Liverpool team returned late on Saturday night from the Midlands after securing the title against West Bromwich Albion, Houlding and the rest of the Liverpool board were there to welcome them at the city's Central Railway Station, along with thousands of supporters. A fife and drum band were ordered to strike up Handel's 'See the Conquering Hero Comes'—the piece played at Liverpool College a decade earlier to mark Everton's first league title celebrations. The choice of song was not uncommon on sporting occasions during the period, but it is not too fanciful to suggest that Houlding had remembered the earlier occasion and knew the significance of its repetition on securing Liverpool's first great trophy. John Houlding had made sure he had the last laugh.

7

DEATH AND LEGACY

John Houlding died at 7:15 a.m. on Monday, 17 March 1902 at the Hotel Pension-Thomson in Cimiez, the South of France resort he had adopted almost as a second home in his declining years. He was aged sixty-nine. When the news reached the city of Liverpool, it was early enough to make the front pages of the city's two evening newspapers, the *Liverpool Express* and the *Liverpool Echo*. Vendors called out the headline to passersby in the late afternoon as they made their way home from work: 'Honest John is Dead'! That evening's *Liverpool Echo* editorial read:

> *Death of John Houlding*
> We regret to learn that Alderman John Houlding died at Nice in the South of France this morning. Alderman Houlding had been in feeble health for some time, but it had been hoped that a trip to the South of France would restore him to convalescence. Last week, however, his condition became so serious that his son and daughter, Councilor William Houlding and Mrs. T. Knowles, were summoned to his bedside. The alderman subsequently sank, and died this morning. [1]

Houlding's demise was not entirely a shock. His later years were plagued with ill health, and though he battled to carry out his normal routine as best he could, his final year was marked by a retreat away from being a public figure. That said, when John Houlding died, it was a significant event for the city.

In the week prior to Houlding's passing, the former Liverpool MP and philanthropist William Rathbone had died. The loss of the patriarch from a famous ship-owning Liverpool family had prompted a period of civic mourning. Rathbone had been associated with a huge amount of charitable work in the city and was the benefactor of a number of public institutions set up for poor relief. John Houlding's passing was met with at least an equal scale of acknowledgment to the one afforded to one of Liverpool's most famous sons. And this was only fitting. In reality, Houlding's importance to local life, politics, and culture far outweighed Rathbone's contribution. Such was the trajectory of Houlding's life; born into an existence on the margins of Liverpool society, the son of a cow keeper from a humble inner-city home, but eclipsing the careers of most of the city's merchant elite. Unquestionably Houlding had been a big beast in the empire's second city and the reaction to his loss was commensurate with that loss.

After the repatriation of Holding's body, his funeral was held four days later at his parish church, St Simon and St Jude's in Anfield, a church he was trustee of, and his burial took place at Everton Cemetery, which he had been largely responsible for creating. The list of groups and organisations in attendance at his funeral was like a roll call of his life and career: the Liverpool Cow Keepers Association; the Liverpool Brewers and Licensed Victuallers Association; the Working Men's Conservative Association; the West Derby Union; the Constitutional Association; the Grand Lodge of England; the Liverpool Carters' Association; the Football Association; the Football League (along with directors of other professional football clubs from England and Scotland—including, significantly and fittingly, Everton FC directors, James Clement Baxter and John C. Brooks); and, of course, the directors and players of Liverpool FC. After the service, the journey from St Simon and St Jude's church to Everton Cemetery went via Liverpool's Anfield Stadium; the club's flags were lowered to half-mast and many of the houses en route, in local tradition, closed their curtains as a mark of respect. King John Houlding had made his final journey through his kingdom.

LEGACY

From today's vantage point, the place to start an appreciation of the legacy of John Houlding would be the huge contribution he made to football. His central role in the building of two famous football organisations is, of course, his ultimate and long-lasting legacy. However, to his contemporaries, the creation of Everton and Liverpool football clubs were not considered the core achievement of Houlding's life. Certainly, in the wake of his passing, his impact as a sports entrepreneur was not the major consideration in the public celebration of his lifetime achievements. Rather, his political influence and his contribution to the social welfare of his fellow citizens were heralded more. And one suspects that John Houlding himself would have agreed with that evaluation. If his proposed autobiography, *From the Dray to St Stephens*,[2] had seen the light of day, it is doubtful that his time at Everton and Liverpool football clubs would have received preeminence within it. Yes, Houlding's sporting associations would have been an important part of his story, but the game simply hadn't reached the stature and importance at that stage to eclipse the public service of a Victorian man who had dedicated his adult life to the city of his birth. It seems appropriate, therefore, to assess Houlding's lasting legacy by turning first to his life as a public servant.

JOHN HOULDING'S SOCIAL AND POLITICAL IMPACT

In the era and area in which he lived, Houlding was a crucially important political figure. He represented the spirit of the age: a man who personified the then-dominant party ideology of Tory Democracy. He was a man from, and of, the people. Working class turned master brewer; Houlding was a man pulled towards Conservatism with a fierce personal commitment to combatting Radicalism: 'The Tory of the Toriest, with an utter detestation of everything savouring of Liberalism and Radicalism', was the description one political commentator settled on for John Houlding.[3] He rapidly rose through the party's ranks, playing a pivotal role in the relations between the Conservative Party and the huge body of working-class men of the north end districts of Liverpool who were vital to maintaining Tory supremacy there and the city as a whole. As a *bona fide* working-class man, his voice had an authenticity few Conservative politicians could match. The chairman of the Working Men's Conservative Association, Sir Archibald Salvidge, acknowledged as much in his final tribute to Houlding: 'No public man was more closely identified with, or took a closer interest in, the workingmen of the city than he did. Some men forgot the ladder which they ascended to high positions, but Alderman Houlding never forgot the workingmen who supported him, and he was true to them, as they were true to him'.[4]

John Houlding had a touch of the 'boss politician' about him. That phenomena certainly could be a dimension to the city's political culture. One Liverpool newspaper, speaking of the local political scene, grandly described such figures as 'the feudal knights of democracy, who hold their faithful adherents in easy thralldom'. Houlding, in particular, it was felt had 'personal magnetism—a psychological gift that some men hold by unknown charm'.[5] Within his own fiefdom of Everton—that vast 'town within a town', with its population approaching one hundred thousand people—a strain of clientelism went hand in hand with the democratic process there. Political horse trading was the norm; favours were done on a nod and a wink for those who could deliver votes. This was machine politics operating in a complex and multicultural cosmopolitan city. Houlding's political legacy, therefore, is partly to do with reinforcing and belonging to a Liverpool political tradition, where big personalities carved out a disproportionate place for themselves in the city's history. The name of John Houlding fits in amongst a list of names who came before and after him, and from across the political spectrum: from Edward Whitley, Houlding's immediate predecessor in Everton; through to T. P. 'Taypay' O'Connor, the Liverpool Irish Nationalist MP for the Scotland Exchange constituency and a contemporary of Houlding's; to the independent Protestant rabble-rousers of the early Edwardian period, such as George Wise; and onto post–Second World War civic leaders like Bessie Braddock, the Labour MP for Liverpool Exchange, and Derek Hatton, the militant deputy leader of the Liverpool Labour Party of the 1980s. On one level, Houlding must be located amongst this pantheon of political and quasipolitical mavericks.

However, there is no question of Houlding being merely a larger-than-life political character who succeeded through self-promotion and a flair for climbing organisational ladders. For decades, he worked painstakingly through a variety of council departments to secure changes to better the lives of others. There can be no doubt that he left his mark on the local state in terms of his commitment to public-health programmes. Houlding's intervention on sanitation, for example, was crucial for the city. As a young man growing up in an era of cholera outbreaks and smallpox epidemics, he was never far away from death due to disease from environmental impact. Overcrowding, poor access to water, and a chronic lack of resources to deal with the city's refuse were the breeding ground for ill health. Houlding's initiative as head of the city council's Health Committee was to introduce cutting-edge machinery to Liverpool in order to deal with the hazard from waste. Known as 'destructors', these were large-scale incinerators of refuse which helped to eliminate the problem of disease emanating from landfill sites located near to population centres (this was the existing way of dealing with the city's waste). Before the twentieth century, most large local authorities baulked at the cost of buying and deploying these machines—the incineration plants and the large and skilled workforce required to operate and maintain them came at a great expense that would have to be passed onto the ratepayers. But Houlding insisted on their introduction in Liverpool, and the city joined with other great metropolises of the world, such as London and New York, which did deploy destructors and were at the forefront of a sanitation revolution.

Houlding's work was not only prodigious as a councilor; he was also the major player in another area of the local state: the rapidly expanding West Derby Union. 'Whether engaged on the Health Committee, the Improvement Committee, or at the West Derby Union, assisting the hospitals or helping the poor and afflicted', The Porcupine journal extolled, '[Houlding] displays the same devotion and zeal that characterised him in conducting his own business'.[6] Houlding had gained a reputation as an expert on Poor Law reform and travelled the country to pass on his experience in making changing national guidelines work. But the Poor Law was also a source of frustration to him: its administration and operation treated poverty and destitution as a statistical problem. It was the outcome of welfare-utilitarianism: determining what the greatest good was for the greatest number when using finite resources levied from residents. Ultimately, that was frustrating to Houlding. As someone who dealt on a daily basis with the enormous pressure brought to bear on the local rates in large urban-industrial communities, he knew that his institution and institutions like it provided a safety net which was being stretched ever wider in order to try and deal with the social consequences of a mobile labour market and cyclical and structural unemployment.

From his own experience, he was well aware of the effects that economic instability could have on family life. Houlding favoured a proactive approach to the alleviation of poverty and so was in the vanguard of introducing social-reform programmes. His work in childcare, and more specifically with orphaned children, was particularly impactful. As a guardian at the West Derby Union, Houlding had had the experience of seeing how children who passed through the workhouse system were ill served by their time in such dire and austere institutions. His contribution to the plight of orphaned children was two-fold: first, by pioneering a project to build a cottage community for orphaned children in the suburban district of Fazakerley; second, by facilitating the emigration of orphaned children to families in Canada for adoption. The Fazakerley Cottage Homes facility Houlding developed took older boys and girls from the workhouse and placed them in a more salubrious environment in order to school them in elementary education, such as reading, writing, and arithmetic, and to teach them the rudiments of a trade that they could use in the future to find employment. Opened in 1889, the Fazakerley Cottage Homes were truly groundbreaking. They contained a large central hall, twenty-four large cottages, a school, a swimming pool, an infirmary, and workshops. It resembled the model garden villages that the industrial philanthropists of the era were building for their workers, such as George Cadbury's Bourneville model village in Birmingham and the Lever Brother's Port Sunlight garden village in the Wirral on Merseyside. Home to six hundred children, the Fazakerley Cottage Homes were, for the standards of the day, a huge step forward in the welfare of orphaned children in the City of Liverpool. They were a credit to Houlding and the West Derby Union. The model experiment was a huge success, housing thousands of children right up until 1959 when the facility was closed as a centre for housing orphans.

Giving workhouse children the chance of escape came also in the form of emigration. Social reformers of the day such as Louisa Birt, a child welfare activist, advocated for the emigration of young orphaned British children to the underpopulated dominions of Canada and Australia as a way of handing them an opportunity for a better life in underpopulated parts of the British Empire. John Houlding was an admirer of the policy. Houlding sent workhouse orphans to both Australia and Canada. Visiting Ontario, Canada in 1885 as part of a follow-up plan to view how children sent there from the West Derby Union had fared, Houlding outlined the philosophy and advantages of this emigration programme, telling the local press: 'Those children, if left in the workhouse, would be brought up for a nameless existence and I intend to recommend more of them be sent to Canada under careful supervision, and placed with private families'.[7]

Obviously, from our vantage point today, we know that the mass emigration of children abroad did not end well for all of those sent away. From the view of the late nineteenth century, however, this was seen to be a progressive way of dealing with the plight of orphaned children, one which offered greater opportunity for a better existence than a life otherwise spent in the densely populated and insalubrious large towns and cities of England.

Houlding's work in sanitation and child welfare perhaps do not provide him with a reformist legacy of extraordinary note. However, taken together they demonstrate that he, as an individual, was a contributor to a broader and emerging social-welfarist political economy in Britain and much of the Western social democracies and that, in Liverpool, he was one of the most active purveyors of social interventionism. Welfarism, and the welfare state, was the coming wave, and Houlding and people like him at a municipal level were at the vanguard of it. Being part of this movement placed Houlding in the tradition of Social Toryism. It would be perhaps claiming too much to describe Houlding as an idealist in this respect—he was, by inclination, a pragmatist—but he would undoubtedly have been influenced by the One Nation Toryism that was identified, in particular, with the iconic Conservative leader of his day, Benjamin Disraeli. Partly as a means to combat the rising tide of socialism, Tories such as Disraeli advocated paternalistic capitalism; a hierarchy of classes, for sure, but where social obligation of the rich towards the poor was at the heart of social relations. Industrialisation had caused dangerous levels of inequality which, if left unchecked, would cause social breakdown, chaos, and very probably lead to the conditions in which revolutionary ferment would thrive. A man like Houlding who feared the rise of radicalism and the overthrow of the established social order, a man who believed in the common sense of reform, became a natural convert to the movement.

SPORTING LEGACY

Houlding was a man who made his mark as a public servant, certainly. But the name John Houlding will forever be most associated with football, and, more particularly, with Liverpool Football Club. The part he played in the rise to prominence of neighbouring Everton FC was substantial, but Liverpool FC was indisputably his creation—an organisation with his personal stamp upon it. It is curious to state then that Houlding's contribution to Liverpool FC has been somewhat (and probably inadvertently) downplayed in much of the official and unofficial literature concerning the first decade or so of the club's existence. There is recognition in these accounts that without John Houlding there would be no Liverpool FC. Houlding is, without contention, afforded the mantle of founding father of the club. But there is a definite underplaying of his crucial role in the development of Liverpool in the period that he was owner. This lack of acknowledgment has been established by the propagation of two notions. First, that Houlding was someone whose primary concern was to be a financial investor in football. Second (and as an outcome of viewing Houlding first and foremost as a speculator), that Houlding was a delegator, and that the men he hired to run the club were more central in establishing its identity. Such notions, though, must be rejected, and Houlding's full legacy reestablished and credited.

In historical accounts of the foundation of Liverpool FC, Houlding is viewed as the club's founder principally in the negative sense of it being the outcome of irresolvable complications at Everton FC which sealed his departure. Rather than the more positive positioning of him as the creative organisational force behind Liverpool FC,[8] Houlding's continued involvement in football after his Everton dismissal is portrayed, essentially, as a businessman maintaining the value of his own asset, having—to use a modern idiom—skin in the game: his ownership of Anfield. In this scenario, figures such as club secretary-cum-manager William Barclay, and more especially, club secretary and director John McKenna (who was, in effect, by the time of Houlding's death, the club's director of football *and* chief executive officer) have been given greater organisational prominence than John Houlding and greater credit for building the foundations of Liverpool FC. It has been said of Barclay's contribution to the club, for example, that 'for the first four years he was everything to Liverpool: kitman, arranger of games, secretary, manager and logistics man. While Houlding sat back and imagined what his new creation could become, Barclay made it happen'.[9] The official history of Liverpool FC, meanwhile, champions the role of John McKenna as Liverpool's true pioneer. 'The handsome, mustachioed' McKenna had eclipsed William Barclay to 'rule Liverpool's affairs'. And not just team affairs—McKenna is also given the credit for the Anfield stadium's overhaul of the mid-

1890s. There is very little mention of John Houlding in any substantial capacity as a key player of the organisation between the period Liverpool were formed in 1892 and up to his death in 1902.[10] The playing up of John McKenna's credentials as 'Mr Liverpool' (and playing down of Houlding's impact) was a feature of the Everton FC Silver Jubilee celebrations in 1929. The then Everton chairman, William Cuff, went to great lengths to elevate the McKenna legacy when recalling Liverpool FC's early history, praising the strides their local rivals had made under the Ulsterman. Referring to the split in the Everton Committee of 1892, Cuff stated, '[Messrs Clayton, Mahon, Baxter, Atkinson and Griffiths] represented the cream of the crop at Anfield Road, but not all the cream of the talent. Some of the cream remained behind and formed the club which is now the Liverpool Football Club, and I refer only to one—Mr John McKenna'.[11]

This unbalanced presentation, though—positioning Houlding as a mere figurehead or bankroller—is unsustainable. It unceremoniously ignores the full imprint Houlding made on Liverpool FC. Not the least of his accomplishments was Houlding's foundation of the club on a firm corporate basis, where investors had control and could expect a reasonable rate of profit. This was a decisive shift away from what had gone on before at Everton FC—a club that retained into the limited company era its structure as a members' club, where power was held at 'rank-and-file' level. We might add to this that Houlding's control of Liverpool FC established the dominant major shareholder figure, which was a novel feature in the Merseyside professional football scene. Modern-day football fans would have no problem in recognising Houlding as a kindred spirit to today's football club owners, who set out the overall tone and direction of a football club which industry experts then carry out as per their instructions. If Houlding similarly leant heavily on the talents of others in the Liverpool hierarchy—using their expertise to carry out his vision of how Liverpool should look and be run—then this was a matter of inspired delegation to men he had handpicked to join him on his new venture, not evidence of a figurehead aloof from the club. Houlding's constant presence in the Liverpool boardroom up to the period of his death underlines this point. In short, Liverpool FC were a club cast in the image of its founder John Houlding, an iconic owner-controller whose all-encompassing grip on that football club made him the very first in a series of giants in its history.

But Houlding's influence over Liverpool FC was not just confined to its governance in a commercial and bureaucratic sense. At the top of the club, amongst the men who controlled it, there was a discernable typology established by Houlding which lasted beyond his death. When Houlding founded the club, he gathered about him men who were socially and politically in lock-step with him. This culture was maintained throughout the Houlding period and it endured for decades. It will be remembered that the 1892 split of Everton FC was laced with bitter in-fighting, and that much of this had its basis in the distinct sociopolitical characteristics of two groups of men who were completely committed and motivated to defeating and expelling the other. The initial intake of men to the Liverpool boardroom was closely overseen by John Houlding, and his preference was to advance men of the same political mindset as him and who shared the same social interests. Active Conservatives and freemasons from the masonic lodges he held sway over found that their path to the Liverpool club boardroom could be a smooth one. Even after Houlding's death in 1902 when the Houlding family's interest in the club was all but ended, the culture of conservatism survived. And Houlding's early determination to preserve the Liverpool boardroom as a bastion for men from commercial backgrounds who were socially and politically conservative remained decisive. The Liverpool director who succeeded Houlding as chairman of the club, Edwin Berry, was one of his protégés, a staunch member of drink-trade defence associations and a Tory councilor for Everton's Breckfield ward. In the wake of the Houlding family exit from the club in 1905, Houlding's son, William; the Conservative councilor for South Walton; and Houlding's son-in-law, Thomas Knowles, a member of the Liverpool Constitutional Association, were replaced by two other dedicated Tories: Edwin Berry's brother Albert Edward Berry, a solicitor for the Working Men's Conservative Association, and Dr Augustus German, secretary of the Ormskirk Conservative Parliamentary Division. In fact, the Liverpool FC boardroom up to and beyond the Second World War sustained this notable link with Liverpool Conservatism. The Liverpool FC board of 1941, for example, included three Tory aldermen: Ralph Knowles Milne, Stanley R. Williams, and George A. Richards. So too was a masonic presence maintained. A number of men with high status within the West Lancashire Provincial Grand Lodge became club directors in the post-Houlding era, including William R. Williams and Richard Martindale. Interestingly, many of the later boardroom members' mother lodges were ones the late John Houlding had major influence in: Anfield Lodge and Everton Lodge.

Undeniably, the club had been cast in Houlding's image. It is inconceivable to view the early decades of Liverpool FC without looking at it through the prism of John Houlding—his character and his preoccupations defined the club. It was this cultural legacy, in all probability, which contributed to the ongoing fractious relations between the boardrooms of Liverpool and Everton football clubs. Culturally speaking, the board at Everton was different to that at Liverpool—more open to men from a variety of occupational, religious, and political backgrounds. Suspicion lingered between the two bodies, and there was little in the way of a rapprochement, even for many years after Houlding had died. Houlding's Liverpool did not sit well with the gentlemen from Goodison Park.

THE HOULDING FAMILY

Houlding's legacy, of course, is also measured in terms of his personal life, and the family he left behind. In John Houlding's case this was his son William, daughter Alice-Margaret, and three grandchildren. His success profoundly affected them all. Just from a financial standpoint alone this was the case. The sale to another local brewery of his large portfolio of public houses (a sale made by Houlding in the last weeks of his life)[12] alone fetched £150,000. Adjusting for inflation, today that figure would amount to in excess of an £18 million inheritance. The control over his brewery business, Houlding's Sparkling Ales, was passed on to and retained by his family until 1914 when it was sold to the Midlands brewery giant Ind Coope and Alsopp for £60,000.[13] And in his last will and testament he left a residual estate of £44,000 to be shared by his son William and daughter Alice-Margaret.

Houlding, then, had bequeathed to his descendants a substantial sum of money by the standards of the period. To put his fortune into context with his peers, Houlding's wealth was greater than the chairman of the Liverpool Docks Board, Thomas Hornby, and that of the well-established cotton merchant Richard Hemelryk; about equal the financial legacy of Edward Clarkson MP, a ship owner in the African trade; though not of the same magnitude (nor anywhere near it) of the brewery magnate Andrew Barclay Walker, who left an estimated estate of £3 million. His son

William's marriage to the daughter and heiress of a Midlands industrialist and Alice-Margaret's marriage into the wealthy and influential Lancastrian Knowles family meant they were both well positioned for a more-than-comfortable existence. But father John's financial legacy allowed them their own independence and credibility amongst such moneyed families. In all likelihood, their father's stature as a wealthy businessman and well-known public figure in Liverpool had brought them into the social orbit of their spouses to begin with.

One other family business the Houlding siblings inherited, of course, was Liverpool FC. The controlling shares in the club passed down to them on their father's death. In the words of the *Liverpool Mercury*, days after Houlding had been laid to rest: 'His place can never be filled, and the Liverpool club is staggering under one of the heaviest blows it has ever received'.[14] The fact that the Houlding family were involved with the club as shareholders and as board members (son William and son-in-law Thomas Knowles were still directors of the club) did not necessarily guarantee continuity. And although dramatic change did not come immediately upon John Houlding's passing, it would in the not-too-distant future.

From the details that are available to us, it seems that William took less of an interest in sport than his father John had done. Unlike John Houlding, a 'self-made' working man, William was the beneficiary of a university education, gaining a degree in Liverpool University before graduating as a barrister at Edinburgh University. William, however, never practiced at law. Instead he took up a managerial position at his father's Liverpool brewery, and also followed in his father's footsteps in representing the Conservative Party as city councilor. It is difficult not to conclude that William's participation in the administration of Liverpool FC was just another way of emulating his father's achievements and remaining close to him. William Houlding remained involved with Liverpool FC for only a short period after his father's death in 1902. He stepped down from his position on the board in 1903 and was soon looking to sell the family stake in the club.

Though no stated reason was given for William Houlding's actions in ending his involvement in the club, we might speculate that Houlding Junior was beginning to diversify his business interests. A 'director of several other companies', he was venturing into other areas of the leisure industry beyond the family's core business interests of brewing and professional football. In 1897, he helped set up and became a director of the theatre company the Liverpool, Leeds, and Hull Empire Palaces Limited,[15] thus entering early into the developing market within the entertainment industry prior to the First World War to provide custom-built theatres in British towns and cities.[16] William Houlding's new company was amalgamated with the larger Moss Empires in 1899, at which point he became a director (and later chairman) of the enlarged organisation which claimed to be 'the largest and most successful chain of variety theatres in the world'.[17] These new theatres, though direct descendants of the free and easies of an earlier period, attempted to provide an air of respectability to the urban entertainment industry: 'Fixed rows of seats replaced the tables and chairs. They were intended to attract families, not just the young and single; to appeal to middle as well as working class; though, of course, safely socially divided. Drink was often not available'.[18] For the university-educated William Houlding, involvement in the theatrical business may well have provided him with a socially superior position to either that of brewer or football club director—a perceived step up and away from the world of his influential father, John Houlding. Additionally, the economic climate was hostile for the brewery industry during this period and the Houlding family's withdrawal from its financial commitments to Liverpool FC may have been influenced also by this factor. The Houlding family's investment in the club may have become an unbearable (or unwanted) financial burden.

Shortly before the end of the 1904–1905 season the board of directors called a public meeting to announce the Houlding family's financial withdrawal from the club. At the meeting, Liverpool Chairman Edwin Berry outlined to the gathered audience of shareholders and its supporters the important role the Houlding family had played in the creation of the club and, crucially, the terms upon which their financial commitment was about to end. The *Liverpool Daily Post* and *Mercury* covered the event:

> He [the chairman] proceeded to sketch the history of the club from the time that Everton went from Anfield to Goodison Park. The late Alderman John Houlding then formed the present club, and he practically bore all the expenses for several years. A large debt accrued, and that money was still owing. It was in name a limited company, but really it was a one man show . . . . There was the difficulty of the load of debt owing to Mr William Houlding, and any profit that was made had to go to the reduction of that, or the payment of the interest. Their present

position was this: they had, roughly speaking, 3,000 shares, and of those, 2,000 were held by the Houlding family, and the other 1,000 by outside people. There was a loan owing to the executors of £10,000 and an overdraft at the bank of £5,000. That overdraft was guaranteed by Alderman Houlding in his lifetime, and had since been continued by his executors. Mr William Holding was approached at the commencement of this year with a view to making the club more popular—that is to say, to put its interests into the hands of the people . . . Mr Houlding said he was willing to meet them, and he proposed, in the first place, to surrender the whole of the shares held by the Houlding family—that was, 2,000—and, secondly, to write off entirely the debt of £10,000 owing to his late father. There still remained the overdraft of £5,000 and it was this sum that Mr Houlding stipulated he should be relieved of. The Chancery Court had consented to the two first named transactions, and the object of the meeting that night was to consider the advisability of raising £6,000 to liquidate the overdraft.[19]

This was a generous offer from the Houlding family: to both surrender their family's stake in the club and write off such a huge debt. The family ownership of the Anfield Stadium was relinquished the following year and the Houlding family interest in Liverpool FC was officially severed.

This disengagement from the club signaled the beginning of a gradual withdrawal of the Houlding family from the city itself. William's work with Moss Empire, a national organisation, meant that time spent in Liverpool was at a premium. Probably for this reason he resigned his position as city councilor for South Walton ward in 1904. This move was, perhaps, a relief to him, as it had been commented that William had more of a 'studious disposition', with 'little liking for public or political prominence';[20] in huge contrast, it might also have accurately been said of this last observation, to his late father. In 1910, William sold Stanley House, the Houlding family home for almost forty years, and for the rest of his years he lived with his family at the sumptuous Kerfield House in the Scottish Borders town of Peebles, and at his other home in Arcachon, a resort near Bordeaux in southwest France. William died in 1930 in Peebles, aged sixty-seven. He was survived by his wife Henrietta, daughter Audrey, and his three grandchildren William, Elizabeth, and Elspeth. Later in life, Audrey married William Millikin-Napier whose father was the Ninth Baronet of Merchiston.

John Houlding's daughter Alice-Margaret left her Newsham Park home in Liverpool soon after the death of her father. She and her husband Thomas Knowles and their sons removed to New Brighton on the Wirral Peninsula—a popular place to live for the wealthy Liverpool middle classes. During the First World War they suffered a terrible blow when their youngest son, William Dowdney Knowles, a captain in the South West Lancashire Regiment, died after contracting tuberculosis in France. Alice-Margaret passed away in 1939, aged eighty. John Houlding, his wife Jane, daughter Alice-Margaret, and grandson William are buried together in their final resting place in Everton Cemetery.

Before concluding the Houlding family story there is the unexplained whereabouts of Isabella Houlding, the youngest daughter of John and Jane, to acknowledge. The 1881 census record for Stanley House identifies her as his fifteen-year-old adopted daughter. Her name, though, is never attributed thereafter in the census records, nor is she ever mentioned in any of the many press reports relating to Houlding's family life. Her fate, having left Stanley House, remains somewhat of a mystery.

WHO WAS JOHN HOULDING?

To one degree or another (and by control of one institution and another), John Houlding changed, or helped to change, the physical and social landscape of Liverpool—and he quite obviously transformed the fortunes of his own family. However, in paying its tribute to the impact John Houlding's life had on the city, the *Liverpool Review* made this interesting distinction: 'Although a man's grit may be testified by his achievements, his inner core is best revealed by the quality of his personality'.[21] So what sort of person can we say John Houlding was?

The view of John Houlding built up in the many thumbnail biographical sketches about him is that he was, above all, a determined and outspoken character; a dynamic man, unwavering and energetic in his pursuit of financial success and personal status. This portrayal rings true. That he knew his own mind is a claim underlined by his contemporaries: 'Alderman Houlding', commented James Thompson, the chairman of the Liverpool Constitutional Association, 'never said what he didn't think, he always said plainly and frankly what he thought'.[22] Houlding's favourite poet was Henry Wadsworth Longfellow, and his favourite Longfellow poem was 'The Psalm of Life'.[23] The poem—a meditation on banishing discouraging thoughts and to strive to fulfill ambition—serves as a reminder that success comes through effort, usually after personal struggle. The final stanza seems particularly appropriate as a code Houlding lived life by:

> Let us, then, be up and doing,
> With a heart for any fate;
> Still achieving, still pursuing,
> Learn to labor and to wait.

It is easy to understand how it moved John Houlding. However, it would be a rather one-dimensional overview of Houlding's character to depict him as being a single-minded man striving for personal gain. From the details of Houlding's life offered in this study, hopefully a more complex understanding of his character has been established.

One of the words which spring to mind when describing John Houlding is 'loyal'. In his personal and public life, his unswerving support could be relied on by family, friends, and colleagues. The loyalty shown to his parents to help out with their struggling dairy business, leaving behind a promising career in the Liverpool customs house to do so; the loyalty he gave to his employer William Clarkson, a man who paid tribute to Houlding's 'faithful and conscientious devotion to duty'[24] over the twenty years of service he gave him and his brewery business; the loyalty to friends he went on to employ at the West Derby Union and in his own brewery; his lifelong loyalty to Thomas McCracken, a man whose company he kept—to the annoyance of the Conservative Party leadership in the city whose side McCracken was a thorn in the side of; and the unswerving loyalty he dedicated to the Conservative cause in Liverpool for over forty years, self-sacrificing his chances of higher office for the sake of party unity.

As we have seen, there was also a generous side to Houlding's character. He devoted a lot of time and money to charitable causes. His name was invariably amongst donors contributing money to funds set up for domestic and foreign disasters. His funding of events for the poorest in his own home town was noteworthy. The aged and the very young were the beneficiaries of his largesse. Perhaps a man with ambition would have been expected to involve themselves in such acts of generosity, but there is a sense that Houlding went above and beyond those expectations.

Houlding can also be described as a traditionalist. A monarchist, he was immensely proud of his yeomanry roots in West Lancashire, and the inherent conservatism of his family shaped the way he viewed the world; it especially informed how he acted in a political sense. On a personal level too Houlding held traditional patriarchal views on the family and the relationship between the sexes. This is captured wonderfully well in a revealing letter to *The Porcupine* journal after his death. It was written by a fellow guest at the Hotel Pension Thomson in Cimiez whom Houlding had become acquainted with in the final weeks of his life. The correspondence, from a Mrs E. A. Jones, gives us an insight into Houlding's mindset. It is reproduced here almost in its entirety:

> We in this hotel only knew Mr Houlding for a few short weeks, yet he made a deep mark on our hearts. Firm and unbending as our English oak, but sound to the core. He was a grand specimen of the men who have made England what she is in the present day. Now his place at the smoking gallery and dinner table are empty. Only a fortnight ago we were attempting a set of quadrilles and a sweet young girl was [unsuccessfully] trying to persuade one of the men to try to dance. Mr Houlding strode across the room, made a curtsy bow, escorted the young lady to her place in the set, then looked around at us quite triumphantly, saying 'I can't stand that, you know.' The same evening when a health was proposed, one of the company offered to touch glasses with him. But he looked straight in the man's face with his clear blue eyes and said 'No, not with a pro-Boer!'. Above all, he is a manly-man. Seven of us went to Villefranche to see the naval battle of flowers.[25] What a pretty sight it was, and the alderman thoroughly enjoyed it from the top of a hotel omnibus. Later on, we descended from our exulted position in quest of tea. The crowd was something terrible, and the manner in which our friend (he would go first) set his shoulders and pushed his way through the French people was a grand sight.

Mrs Jones went on,

> Nothing escaped his eyes. One evening I remember we had fresh arrivals in the shape of a very fascinating little French woman and her husband. Whilst I was busy with the pots, Mr Houlding bent his head close to mine and whispered 'That woman has talked all dinner time and that poor beggar has never opened his mouth'. One thing he has little patience with, he said, is wives who govern their husbands, and

husbands who allow themselves to be governed. I would go on much
longer writing about Alderman Houlding, but I will refrain.[26]

In parts charming, chivalrous, and chauvinistic, Houlding would have
approximated to what most considered a gentleman by the standards of
the day. The words of his admirer, Mrs Jones, concerning his character
though perhaps reinforced a misconception about Houlding as a man who
relied on what would be described today as 'social skills' or 'people
skills' rather than intellect. 'A fine student of mankind' is how one observer described Houlding.[27]

Respected he may have been, but he was constantly underestimated.
The *Liverpool Review* accounted for his success as being down to 'the
solidity of his character'; and the *Liverpool Daily Post* stressed his 'com-
monsense and honesty'.[28] The projected image of Houlding is one of a
man guided in his actions through instinct, not especially by his learned-
ness. It would be unwise to completely rebuff this representation. Certainly, in much of his public life he appears to have been a man whose
decision making was based upon social observation and character assessment rather than ideology and political science. However, this is not a
balanced assessment of Houlding's capabilities. Leaving aside his organisational genius in the local state, and his transformation of the cultural
topography of the city of Liverpool through his sports entrepreneurship,
the implied dismissal of Houlding's sophistication and intellect sits uncomfortably with his well-established thirst for international travel, his
love of poetry, his mastery of the arcane laws and procedures of the world
of master freemasonry, and by his bilingualism. Other graduates of his
alma mater, the Liverpool College, young men from moneyed backgrounds who were his political peers in the city of Liverpool in later life
had, as of right, the choice to go on to a good university and the chance to
develop their intellect to the full. John Houlding though had the more
pressing matter of helping his family survive by taking up paid work at
the port of Liverpool. The denial of the higher education that most of his
peers took for granted adds context to Houlding's personal intellectual
development and, indeed, to his many achievements.

However, we must temper our eulogies. John Houlding was a man
with character flaws too. An admirer of Houlding's once declared that his
political opponents always acknowledged his fairness and propriety in the
council chamber.[29] However, those same opponents also knew him to be

a man not to cross swords with. To use football jargon, Houlding often played the man and not the ball. *Ad hominem* attacks on the personal integrity of challengers to his council seat bears testimony to this. The weapon of choice he most readily reached for in order to undermine was his accusation that opponents were mere puppets, whose 'wire-pullers' were 'the radicals'. Houlding could also on occasion act out of spite. His conduct during the Everton Football Club split in 1892 and, more especially, its aftermath, revealed this side of Houlding's personality. The part he played in the souring of relations between Liverpool and Everton seems clear enough. His obstruction to the removal of crucial stadium infrastructure from Anfield owned by the members of Everton FC and his (almost certain) central role in reporting Everton to the police for the sale of lottery tickets in aid of Stanley Hospital was an evening up of scores that should have been beneath Houlding. But he compounded this ill-advised and boorish behavior towards Everton by apparently targeting an individual on Everton's board of directors, William R. Clayton; in one instance attempting to persuade Clayton's employer (and Constitutional Association colleague) William Dwerryhouse to dismiss the Everton man from his position. This was an accusation that Houlding denied, but there was undoubtedly a fractious relationship between the two men.[30]

* * *

In his comprehensive tome of nineteenth- and twentieth-century Liverpool, *Democracy and Sectarianism: A Social and Political History of Liverpool*, author Philip Waller notes the contribution made by John Houlding as follows: 'Hotel proprietor; brewer; prominent in Everton public life; Lord Mayor; football enthusiast'.[31] All of which is factually correct. However, and as we have seen, there was much more breadth and scope to Houlding's life and career than this, and the soubriquet Waller saddled Houlding with of 'parochial patriot' is an ill-fitting and slightly dismissive one. What John Houlding achieved went way beyond the confines of the district associated with him. He had a major impact on the whole of Liverpool via his influence over the political life of the city and the health and welfare measures he instigated; his profile within the hierarchy of freemasonry extended his reputation beyond Liverpool nationally; and his pioneering of professional football organisations on Merseyside is a cultural contribution which has left a global imprint. This said—and though 'King John of Everton' is a description that obscures the scale of John Houlding's legacy—it was a title conferred on him by the people he served, and he himself would have been satisfied with that.

NOTES

INTRODUCTION

1. Liverpool CEO Peter Moore, speaking to Forbes: 'Liverpool FC Eyes US Market This Summer in International Champions Cup', 31 May 2018, https://www.forbes.com/sites/setheverett/2018/05/31/liverpool-fc-eyes-u-s-market-this-summer-in-international-champions-cup/#70124fc45352.

2. Tony Lane, *Liverpool: City of the Sea*, 30.

3. Quote from the chairman of English Heritage, Sir Neil Cossens: 'Heritage Map for Changing City', BBC News, 19 March 2002, http://news.bbc.co.uk/1/hi/england/1881661.stm.

1. FROM TENTERDEN STREET
TO ANFIELD ROAD

1. Figures from Richard Lawton's 'The Population of Liverpool in the Mid-Nineteenth Century' (based on sample of fourteen thousand).

2. An increase from twenty-four thousand in 1801 to sixty-one thousand in 1841. Figures taken from the council wards of Vauxhall, St Paul's, and Exchange in P. Laxton, 'Liverpool in 1801: A Manuscript Return for the First National Census of Population', the Historical Society of Lancashire and Cheshire, vol. 130, 1980, table 5, p. 93.

3. *Liverpool Courier*, 18 March 1902.

4. A moment remembered by Houlding in interview with *The Porcupine*, 23 December 1893.

5. 'As Bad as Victorian Times', https://straightstatistics.fullfact.org/article/bad-victorian-times.

6. Sheila Marriner, *The Economic and Social Development of Merseyside*, 31–32.

7. *Illustrated London News*, 15 May 1886, quoted in David Beckingham's *The Licensed City*, 2.

8. 'The Brewer's Drayman', Debrett Ancestry Research, https://debrettancestryresearch.com/the-brewers-drayman/.

9. Walter A. Riley, 'Brewing Labour Problems', 145.

10. *The Porcupine*, 23 December 1893.

11. *Liverpool Courier*, 18 March 1902.

12. Jeffrey Williams, 'Great Britain Nominal Annual Earnings for Various Occupations in England and Wales', 1982, http://www.pierre-marteau.com/currency/indices/uk-03.html.

13. *Liverpool Mercury*, 29 January 1887.

14. Tony Mason, *Oxford Dictionary of National Biography* (entry for John Houlding), https://www.oxforddnb.com/view/10.1093/ref:odnb/9780198614128.001.0001/odnb-9780198614128-e-56195.

15. *Liverpool Mercury*, 28 August 1866.

16. Alistair Mutch, 'Magistrates and Public House Managers: 1840–1914: Another Case of Liverpool Exceptionalism'.

17. Neil Collins, 'Politics and Elections in Nineteenth-Century Liverpool', 158.

18. Philip Waller, *Democracy and Sectarianism*, 108.

19. Collins, 'Politics and Elections in Nineteenth-Century Liverpool', 158.

20. David Beckingham, *The Licensed City: Regulating Drink in Liverpool*, https://www.cam.ac.uk/research/features/the-capital-of-drinking-did-19th-century-liverpool-deserve-its-reputation.

21. *Liverpool Courier*, 18 March 1902.

22. *Liverpool Mercury*, 7 July 1874.

23. *Liverpool Echo*, 11 November 1990.

24. *Liverpool Mercury*, 5 January 1885.

25. *Liverpool Mercury*, 2 June 1882; *Liverpool Mercury*, 8 November 1883.

2. CONQUERING EVERTON

1. Sir J. A. Picton, *Memorials of Liverpool*, 364.

2. Data taken from author's own samples taken from Census Enumerator Reports 1881 and 1891.

3. Picton, *Memorials of Liverpool*, 353.

4. Philip Waller, *Democracy and Sectarianism*, 12.

5. *Liverpool Mercury*, 14 July 1885.

6. *Liverpool Mercury*, 28 March 1890.

7. Quote from report in *The Porcupine* about the creation of the first Liverpool Working Men's Conservative Association in the late 1860s, 17 July 1869.

8. Waller, *Democracy and Sectarianism*, 142.

9. Ibid., 32–33.

10. Ibid., 286.

11. Ibid., 32.

12. Report of Houlding's connection to this lodge in *Liverpool Mercury*, 14 July 1885.

13. *Liverpool Daily Post*, 15 February 1883.

14. D. Kennedy and M. Collins, 'Community Politics in Liverpool', 768.

15. *Liverpool Mercury*, 27 December 1880.

16. *Walsall Advertiser*, 29 October 1898.

17. *Liverpool Mercury*, 24 June 1881.

18. *Liverpool Athletic News*, 19 October 1886.

3. FROM HERO TO VILLAIN

1. Keates, *History of the Everton Football Club*.

2. Ibid., 150.

3. *Cricket and Football Field*, 12 December 1887.

4. *Liverpool Daily Post*, 27 October 1891.

5. David France and David Prentice, *Virgin Blues*, 17.

6. Ibid., 22.

7. *Liverpool Mercury*, 9 May 1891.

8. France and Prentice, *Virgin Blues*, 6. Rule 2 of club rules (from 1888–1889 Everton FC Management Committee Meeting Minutes).

9. Committee membership taken from *Liverpool Courier*, 13 October 1891, and *Liverpool Daily Post*, 5 February 1892.

10. *Liverpool Daily Post*, 21 October 1891.

11. Everton FC minute book 1887–1891, Everton Collection, http://www.evertoncollection.org.uk/object?id=796+EFC%2f1%2f1%2f1. See also Keates, *History of the Everton Football Club*, 40.

12. See, for example, *Liverpool Review*, 'Lively Proceedings Expected at Next Everton Football Club AGM', 25 May 1889 and 'Everton Football Club', 1 June 1889.

13. Everton FC Minutes, 18 June 1888, Everton Collection.

14. See France and Prentice, *Virgin Blues*, 11 and 20; Keates, *History of the Everton Football Club*, 37–38.

15. France and Prentice, *Virgin Blues*, 26.

16. *Liverpool Review*, 'Lively Proceedings Expected at Next Everton Football Club AGM', 25 May 1889.

17. *Liverpool Review*, 'Everton Football Club', 1 June 1889.

18. France and Prentice, *Virgin Blues*, 28.

19. *Liverpool Courier*, 16 March 1892.

4. POLITICAL AMBITIONS CHECKED

1. *Liverpool Mercury*, 7 April 1890.

2. *Liverpool Mercury*, 27 October 1891.

3. *Liverpool Mercury*, 23 October 1891.

4. *Liverpool Mercury*, 11 January 1895.

5. Quoted in Phillip Waller, *Democracy and Sectarianism*, 106.

6. *Liverpool Mercury*, 29 October 1891.

7. David Beckingham, *The Licensed City*, 170.

8. *Liverpool Mercury*, 23 October 1891.

9. *Liverpool Mercury*, 30 October 1891.

10. Ibid.

11. *Liverpool Mercury*, 17 October 1891.

12. *Liverpool Courier*, 3 November 1891.

13. *Liverpool Courier*, 23 October 1891.

14. *Liverpool Mercury*, 24 October 1891.

15. *Liverpool Daily Post*, 20 October 1891, letter from J. W. McGovern of Liverpool Trades Council.

16. Ibid.

17. *Liverpool Courier*, 24 October, 1891; *Liverpool Daily Post*, 13 April 1892.

18. *Liverpool Mercury*, 3 November 1891.

19. Ibid.

20. *Liverpool Courier*, 26 January 1892.

21. *Liverpool Courier*, 22 January 1892.

22. *Liverpool Courier*, 25 January 1892.

23. J. A. Klapas, 'Geographical Aspects of Religious Change, 1837–1901', Appendix 3a.

24. *Liverpool Courier*, 22 January 1892.

25. *Liverpool Mercury*, 26 January 1892.

26. *Liverpool Mercury*, 27 January 1892.

27. *Liverpool Mercury*, 2 February 1892.

28. *Liverpool Mercury*, 4 February 1892.

29. *Liverpool Mercury*, 5 February 1892.

30. Quoted by Philip Waller, 'Forwood, Sir Arthur Bower, First Baronet (1836–1898)', *Oxford Dictionary of National Biography*, https://www.oxforddnb.com/view/10.1093/ref:odnb/9780198614128.001.0001/odnb-9780198614128-e-38693?rskey=CalhyU&result=2.

31. *Liverpool Mercury*, 6 February 1892.

32. *Liverpool Mercury*, 15 February 1892.

33. Ibid.

34. Thomas McCracken is recorded amongst the close company of friends Houlding took with him to a preseason club sports day at Ormskirk, Lancashire in August. The other men mentioned were club directors or officers and it is strongly suggestive that McCracken was also involved with the club in some capacity. *Liverpool Mercury*, 24 August 1894.

35. *Liverpool Mercury*, 26 December 1892.

36. *Liverpool Mercury*, 11 February 1890 and 27 January 1892.

37. John Williams, *Red Men, Liverpool Football Club—The Biography*, 60.

5. THE FOUNDATION OF LIVERPOOL FOOTBALL CLUB

1. *Liverpool Daily Post*, 17 October 1891.

2. *Liverpool Daily Post*, 25 January 1892.

3. George Mahon—Everton's first chairman—was a committee member of Walton Liberal Association; Dr William Whitford was chairman of Everton and Kirkdale Liberal Association; William R. Clayton was the chairman of Formby Liberal Association; James Clement Baxter was Liberal city councilor for St Anne's ward; Alfred Riley Wade was a member of Exchange Liberal Association. Sources: for Clayton, see Southport Liberal Association, Annual Reports, 1899–1930; Executive Committee Meeting Minutes, 1880–1930; for Baxter, see Liverpool City Council Annual Committee and Sub-Committee Reports, 1906–1921; Baxter's funeral report, *Liverpool Mercury*, 28 January 1928; for Mahon, see *Bootle Times*, 11 January and 1 March 1889 for reports of Walton Liberal Association meetings.

4. *Liverpool Daily Post*, 19 March 1892.

5. *Liverpool Review*, 'Open Letter to Dr Whitford' by "Diogenes",' 7 November 1896; *The Porcupine*, 'People Who Are Talked About: Dr William Whitford', 26 December 1896.

6. B. G. Orchard, *Liverpool's Legion of Honour*, 490 (1893). George Mahon biographical sketch: 'George Mahon, 1853–1908', https://georgema-hon.webs.com.

7. Everton Committee Meeting report and letter to editor in *Liverpool Daily Post*, 'Everton Football Club', 3 March 1892, p. 7 and 'The Difficulties of the Everton Football Club', 16 March 1892, p. 6.

8. *Bootle Times*, 'Sir David Radcliffe Disqualified', 12 January 1889, p. 5.

9. *Liverpool Courier*, 4 March 1892; *Liverpool Courier*, 18 February 1892; *Liverpool Courier*, 30 January 1892.

10. *Liverpool Mercury*, 16 March 1892.

11. *Liverpool Mercury*, 21 March 1892.

12. *Liverpool Daily Post*, 30 March 1892.

13. *Liverpool Daily Post*, 30 May 1892.

14. See Liverpool Football Club and Athletics Ground Company Limited, Director and Shareholder Registers, Articles and Memorandum of Association, Company File Number BT31/35668.

15. Everton Football Club Company Limited, Director and Shareholder Registers, Articles and Memorandum of Association. Company File Number BT31/36624.

16. Accessions Box (File D), Liverpool Record Office.

17. See *Athletic News*, 22 May 1899 and 14 August 1899.

18. *Liverpool Mercury*, 27 August 1894.

19. *Liverpool Mercury*, 5 September 1892.

20. *Athletic News*, 22 May 1893.

21. Quoted in John Williams, *Red Men, Liverpool Football Club—The Biography*, 57.

22. *Liverpool Courier*, 24 May 1892.

23. *Liverpool Echo*, 10 December 1892.

24. *Liverpool Daily Post*, 23 January 1893.

25. *Liverpool Review* quoted by Williams, *Red Men, Liverpool Football Club—The Biograph*, 55.

26. *Liverpool Review*, 25 January 1895.

27. *Liverpool Mercury*, 22 August 1892.

6. JOHN HOULDING,
LORD MAYOR OF LIVERPOOL

1. *Liverpool Courier*, 2 November 1896.

2. *Liverpool Mercury*, 18 June 1895.

3. *Liverpool Mercury*, 12 February 1897.

4. *Liverpool Echo*, 17 March 1902.

5. *The Era*, 11 March 1893.

6. *Liverpool Mercury*, 21 September 1897.

7. *Liverpool Mercury*, 1 November 1897.

8. Ibid.

9. *Liverpool Mercury*, 1 November 1897.

10. *Liverpool Mercury*, 27 September 1897.

11. *Liverpool Mercury*, 27 October 1897.

12. *Liverpool Mercury*, 24 September 1897.

13. *Liverpool Mercury*, 27 October 1897.

14. *Liverpool Mercury*, 30 October 1897.

15. *Liverpool Mercury*, 1 November 1897.

16. *Liverpool Mercury*, 9 November 1897.

17. *Liverpool Mercury*, 30 October 1897.

18. *Liverpool Mercury*, 1 November 1897; *Liverpool Mercury*, 6 November 1897; *Liverpool Mercury*, 11 November 1897.

19. *Liverpool Mercury*, 10 November 1897.

20. Ibid.

21. Ibid.

22. *The Porcupine*, 19 November 1898.

23. *Liverpool Mercury*, 12 January 1887.

24. *Liverpool Mercury*, 19 November 1897.

25. *Liverpool Mercury*, 19 July 1877.

26. Everton Lodge: Albert Edward Berry, Edwin Berry, Thomas Bush, John Houlding, Francis Minshall, John James Ramsey, James Herbert Troop; Anfield Lodge: William Coward Briggs, Thomas Knowles, Alexander Nisbet, George Patterson, Richard H. Webster. Grand Lodge of England Country Returns.

27. *Liverpool Mercury*, 1 May 1900 and 3 May 1900.

28. *Liverpool Mercury*, 10 March 1900.

7. DEATH AND LEGACY

1. *Liverpool Echo*, 17 March 1902.

2. A biography John Houlding wished to write, a fact which he confided in his old friend Thomas McCracken. See *Liverpool Mercury*, 15 February 1892. The title referred to the rise of Houlding from a brewer's drayman to (where he hoped his final career destination would be) St Stephen's Hall—the chamber at Westminster where parliament once sat.

3. *Liverpool Echo*, 25 April 1925.

4. *Liverpool Courier*, 25 March 1902.

5. *Liverpool Echo*, 25 April 1925.

6. *The Porcupine*, 22 March 1902.

7. *Liverpool Mercury*, 18 August 1885.

8. See, for example, Jeff Goulding, *Red Odyssey: Liverpool FC 1892–2017*, chapter 1.

9. Michael Foley, 'Piecing Together Story of Liverpool's Forgotten Founding Father', *Sunday Times*, 11 June 2017, https://www.thetimes.co.uk/article/piecing-together-story-of-liverpools-forgotten-founding-father-39cln0qhc.

10. Stephen F. Kelly, *Liverpool: The Official Illustrated History*, 14–17.

11. *Liverpool Echo*, 24 April 1929.

12. *Liverpool Echo*, 20 March 1902.

13. By 1939, Houlding's name was dropped by the acquiring company and the Houlding brand ceased to exist. Lesley Richmond and Alison Turton, *The Brewing Industry*, 187.

14. *Liverpool Mercury*, 24 March 1902.

15. *Liverpool Daily Post*, 21 January 1930.

16. W. Hamish Fraser and R. J. Morris, *People and Society in Scotland*, 257.

17. G. J. Mellor, *The Northern Music Hall*, 121.

18. Fraser and Morris, *People and Society in Scotland*, 257.

19. *Liverpool Daily Post*, 23 February 1905.

20. *Liverpool Echo*, 25 April 1928.

21. *Liverpool Review*, 22 March 1902.

22. *Liverpool Courier*, 25 March 1902.

23. Houlding's admiration for the poem is mentioned in *The Porcupine*, 22 March 1902.

24. *Liverpool Courier*, 25 March 1902.

25. A parade in the harbor to mark the end of the Riviera season, where crew and passengers on board vessels throw thousands of flowers at spectators lining the wharves; the 'battle' occurring when the spectators throw the flowers back at the vessels.

26. *The Porcupine*, 22 March 1902.

27. Ibid.

28. *Liverpool Review*, 22 March 1902; *Liverpool Daily Post*, 22 March 1902.

29. *The Porcupine*, 22 March 1902.

30. *Liverpool Courier*, 16 March 1892.

31. Philip J. Waller, *Democracy and Sectarianism*.

BIBLIOGRAPHY

NEWSPAPERS AND PERIODICALS (LIVERPOOL RECORD OFFICE)

Bootle Times
Cricket and Football Field
Liverpool Athletic and Dramatic News
Liverpool Brewers and Victuallers Journal (British Newspaper Library, Collindale, London)
Liverpool Courier
Liverpool Daily Post
Liverpool Echo
Liverpool Mercury
Liverpool Review
The Porcupine

BOOKS

Accessions Box (File D), Liverpool Record Office. Everton and Liverpool football club assorted club papers (held at Liverpool Record Office).
Aked, C. F. *England Free and Sober* (self-published, Liverpool, 1897).
Allied Breweries (Houlding Brewery Company Shareholder Registers). Burton-on-Trent.
Armstrong, R. A. *The Deadly Shame of Liverpool* (Liverpool: self-published, 1890).
Barnes, Tommy. *Third Time Lucky: Bootle Football Club* (Liverpool: Countyvise, 1988).
Beckingham, David. *The Licensed City: Regulating Drink in Liverpool, 1830–1920* (Liverpool: Liverpool University Press, 2017).
Belchem, John. *Merseypride: Essays in Liverpool Exceptionalism* (Liverpool: Liverpool University Press, 2000).

Bolger, Paul. *Edwardian A–Z and Directory of Liverpool and Bootle British Labour Statistics: Historical Abstract, 1886–1968*. Her Majesty's Stationary Office (HMSO, 1971).

Burke, Thomas. *A Catholic History of Liverpool* (Liverpool: Wentworth Press, 2016).

Census Reports, England and Wales, 1841, 1851, 1861, 1871, 1881, 1891, 1901.

Collins, Neil. *Politics and Elections in Nineteenth-Century Liverpool* (Aldershot: Routledge, 1994).

Collins, Tony, and Wray Vamplew. *Mud, Sweat and Beers: A Cultural History of Sport and Alcohol* (Oxford: Berg, 2002).

Davies, Sam. *Liverpool Labour: Social and Political Influences on the Development of the Labour Party in Liverpool, 1900–1939* (Keele: Keele University Press, 1996).

Everton Collection. Minute Books. Liverpool Record Office.

Everton Football Club Company Limited. Director and Shareholder Registers, Articles and Memorandum of Association. Company File Number BT31/36624. Companies House, Cardiff.

France, David, and Prentice, David. *Virgin Blues: 100 Seasons at the Top* (Whitham: Skript Publishing, 2003).

Fraser, W. Hamish, and R. J. Morris. *People and Society in Scotland: Vol. 2, 1830–1914* (Edinburgh: John Donald, 1990).

Goulding, Jeff. *Red Odyssey: Liverpool FC 1892–2017* (Worthing: Pitch Publishing, 2018).

Gourvish T. R., and R. G. Wilson. *The British Brewing Industry: 1830–1980* (Cambridge: Cambridge University Press, 1994).

Grand Lodge of England. Country Returns. Grand Lodge Library, London.

Gutzke, David W. *Protecting the Pub: Brewers and Publicans Against Temperance* (Woodbridge: Royal Historical Society, 1989).

Hawkins, K. H., and C. H. Pass. *The Brewing Industry: A Study in Industrial Organisation and Public Policy* (Portsmouth: Heinemann Educational Books, 1979).

Horne, John. B., and Thomas Bruce Maund. *Liverpool Transport*: Vol. 1, 1830–1900 (Glossop: Senior Publications, 1975).

Houlding, John. Will and Grant, Registry for Grants, Wills and Probate Index, Principal Registry of the Family Division. High Holborn, London.

Jones, John Richard. *The Welsh Builder on Merseyside: Annals and Lives* (Liverpool: self-published, 1946).

Keates, Thomas. *The History of the Everton Football Club*, second edition (Trowbridge: Desert Island, 1998).

Kelly, Stephen F. *Forever Everton: The Official History of Everton FC* (London: McDonald, 1987).

———. *You'll Never Walk Alone: The Official Illustrated History of Liverpool FC* (London: Queen Anne Press, 1988).

———. *Liverpool: The Official Illustrated History* (London: Hamlyn, 1996).

Kennedy, David. *A Social and Political History of Everton and Liverpool Football Clubs: The Split, 1878–1914* (Abingdon: Routledge, 2016).

Kennedy, David, and M. Collins. '"Community Politics in Liverpool" and the Governance of Professional Football in the Late Nineteenth Century'. *Historical Journal* 49, no. 3 (2019): 761–88.

Klapas, J. A. 'Geographical Aspects of Religious Change in Victorian Liverpool, 1837–1901' (unpublished MA thesis, University of Liverpool, 1977).

Knight, Steven. *The Brotherhood: The Secret World of Freemasonry* (London: Harper Perennial, 1983).

Lane, Tony. *Liverpool: City of the Sea* (Liverpool: Liverpool University Press, 1997).

Lawton, Richard. 'The Population of Liverpool in the Mid-Nineteenth Century'. *Transactions of the Historical Society of Lancashire and Cheshire* 107 (1955): 89–120.

Laxton, P. 'Liverpool in 1801: A Manuscript Return for the First National Census of Population'. *The Historical Society of Lancashire and Cheshire* 130 (1981): 73–113.

Lewis, Robert W. 'The Genesis of Professional Football: Bolton-Blackburn-Darwen, the Centre of Innovation, 1878–85'. *The International Journal of the History of Sport* 14, no. 1 (1997): 21–54.

Liverpool Constitutional Association. Board Minutes and Annual Reports of County Associations, 1860–1947. Liverpool Record Office.

Liverpool Council Liquor Licensing Records (Annual). Register of Licenses Other Than Victuallers. Liverpool Record Office.

Liverpool Football Club and Athletics Ground Company Limited. Director and Shareholder Registers, Articles and Memorandum of Association, Company File Number BT31/35668. Companies House, Cardiff.

Liverpool Football Club Official Matchday Programmes. London: Collindale British Newspaper Library, Liverpool Record Office.

Liverpool Parliamentary Debating Society Papers, 1900–1945.

Marriner, Sheila. *The Economic and Social Development of Merseyside* (London: Croom Helm, 1982).

Mellor, G. J. *The Northern Music Hall* (Newcastle: Frank Graham, 1970).

Munro, Alasdair. 'Tramway Companies in Liverpool, 1859–1897'. *Transactions of the Historic Society of Lancashire and Cheshire* 119 (1967): 181–207.

Mutch, Alistair. 'Magistrates and Public House Managers: 1840–1914: Another Case of Liverpool Exceptionalism'. *Journal of Northern History* 40, no. 2 (2013): 325–42.

Orchard, B. G. *Liverpool's Legion of Honour* (Birkenhead: self-published, 1893).

Orrell Brewing Syndicate Company Limited. Company File Number BT31/4962/33147. Kew, London: Public Record Office.

Orrell, John. Will and Grant, Registry for Grants, Wills and Probate Index, Principal Registry of the Family Division. High Holborn, London.

Picton, J. A. *Memorials of Liverpool* (Liverpool: self-published, 1903).

Pooley, Colin G. 'Migration, Mobility and Residential Areas in Nineteenth-Century Liverpool' (unpublished PhD diss., University of Liverpool, 1978).

Rees, Ben D. *Local and Parliamentary Politics in Liverpool From 1800–1911* (New York: The Edwin Mellen Press Limited, 1999).

Rees, R. 'The Development of Physical Recreation in Liverpool During the Nineteenth Century' (unpublished MA thesis, University of Liverpool, 1968).

Richardson, P. E. 'The Development of Professional Football on Merseyside, 1878–1894' (unpublished MA thesis, University of Lancaster, 1983).

Richmond, Lesley, and Alison Turton, eds. *The Brewing Industry: A Guide to Historical Records* (Manchester: Manchester University Press, 1990).

Riley, Walter A. 'Brewing Labour Problems'. *Journal of the Institute of Brewing* 25, no. 3 (1919): 141–70.

Roberts, John. *Everton: The Official Centenary History* (London: Mayflower, 1978).

Roberts, Keith Daniel. *Liverpool Sectarianism: The Rise and Demise*. (Liverpool: Liverpool University Press, 2017).

Salvidge, Stanley. *Salvidge of Liverpool: Behind the Political Scene 1890–1928* (Liverpool: Hodder and Stoughton, 1934).

Shiman, Lilian L. *Crusade Against Drink in Victorian England* (London: Palgrave McMillan, 1988).

Taplin, Eric L. 'The Liverpool Trades Council, 1880–1914'. *Bulletin of the North West Labour History Society,* no. 3 (1976).

Taylor, E. R. *Methodism and Politics, 1791–1851* (Cambridge: Cambridge University Press, 1935).

Tischler, Steven. *Footballers and Businessmen: The Origins of Professional Soccer in England* (New York: Holmes and Meier, 1980).

Waller, Phillip J. *Democracy and Sectarianism: A Political and Social History of Liverpool* (Liverpool: Liverpool University Press, 1981).

West Derby Union. Board of Guardian and General Purposes Committee Meeting Reports. Liverpool Record Office.

Whittingham-Jones, Barbara. *Down With the Orange Caucus* (Liverpool: self-published, 1936).

Williams, John. *Red Men, Liverpool Football Club—The Biography* (Edinburgh: Mainstream, 2010).

Williams, John, et al. *Passing Rhythms: Liverpool FC and the Transformation of Football* (Manchester: Berg, 2002).

Winskill, P. T. *History of the Temperance Movement in Liverpool and District* (Liverpool: Joseph Thomas, 1887).

INDEX

ABOUT THE AUTHOR

David Kennedy is a football industry researcher. He is the author and coauthor of a number of books and articles related to European football club governance and fan culture. A historian, he takes a particular interest in the formation and development of Merseyside football.